JUST ACE IT

TREVOR CONNER

JUST ACE IT

CONTROLLING LIFE'S UNCONTROLLABLES

HEARTS & MINDS

ISBN 978-1-7339954-0-5 (PAPERBACK)

Just ACE It: Controlling Life's Uncontrollables

First Printing, 2019
Hearts & Minds

This book is for each athlete out there, trying to be their best.

It was written for all who have inspired me over the past 8 years. I pray that it may it be a spark of continued inspiration for every person who reads it.

ACKNOWLEDGMENTS

To my father and mother, thank you for always believing in me and encouraging me to live a life full of goals with a heart filled with passion, perseverance, and a fire to chase them. I love you both.

To all the countless athletes, families, teachers, co-workers, military personnel, and mentors that have been present in my life and career to this point, I thank you for the opportunity in our time together to listen, learn, teach, and love.

Incredible shout out of thanks and praise to Paul, Esbe, Carlie, Sonia, Victoria, and Annabelle of the CreateNonfiction.com team. Without your brilliant company believing in me, my story, and my mission, and helping me share it with the world, I would still be in wishful thinking mode.

Special shout out and thank you to Esbe van Heerden for supporting me through this entire book writing journey. You're the BEST! From the bottom of my heart, thank you!

To Winston. Thank you for introducing me to a 2 Timothy 2:2 life years ago and for helping me connect the dots of ACE to a bigger purpose and reason. Your willingness to lead me in the Word and disciple me, means more than measure. Phileo love.

To my son Gabriel, I pray my son that you can learn, lead, and live a life filled with the simplicity and bedrock foundation of ACE where others all around you will take notice that you live a Romans 12:2 life.

To my best friend and wife Erica, you're such a blessing, and an inspiration to me. Your continuous support and belief in me and my mission to impact others helps fuel my fire when things get tough. I cannot thank you enough. I love you. Unconditionally.

Lastly, I want to thank God. For giving an endless amount of love, joy, peace, patience, kindness, goodness, faithfulness, gentleness, and self-control whenever one asks. You are an awesome God whom knows no boundaries or limits and whom is faithful for any who puts their trust in you fully (Romans 10:9).

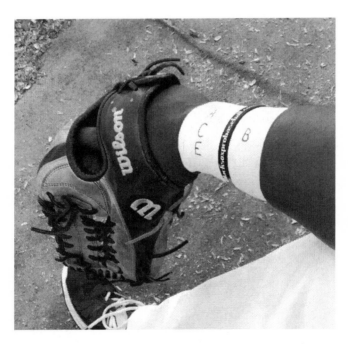

"Living and playing with ACE...stay zeroed"
Photo Credit—an unnamed professional baseball player 2019.

CONTENTS

INTRODUCTION

You won't like what I'm about to say—but it's the foundation of everything that follows in this book.

Most things in your life—almost everything, in fact—are out of your control.

This may not seem that controversial—we've all heard sayings like, *you can't control others, you can only control yourself*—but I really want to emphasize this.

Because the fact is, we tend to act like we're in control—whether we're willing to admit it or not. We think to ourselves, *if I say the right thing, I can get that person to like me. If I get good grades, I can get into the school where I want to go. If I work hard enough at my job, I'll get promoted.*

Humans fundamentally crave control, and we are always instinctively trying to control the world around us. The world is scary and unpredictable, so we create this illusion that we control parts of it. We create a box, made of the things we think we control, and the rituals we've invented to control them, and we stay inside, where it feels safe. But life has a way of throwing curveballs, and before you know it, that sense of control is ripped from you by some disastrous event where you're left feeling completely devastated.

That's life, you might be thinking. *Things happen.*

Things do happen! But that pain and devastation that we experience when something doesn't go our way—that's not caused by life. It's caused by our illusion of control. Thinking you're in control only sets you up for pain and disappointment when you inevitably learn the hard way, that you're not.

A professional baseball player who was drafted in the 2018 MLB draft straight out of high school came to me distraught. You may be thinking, someone who had the opportunity to chase the pro ball career at 18-years-old, what possibly could he have been through?! The reality was, he had already come through tremendous adversity: his mother had died of breast cancer when he was just 12, and her dying wish was for him to make it to the major leagues. What unrelenting pressure that must have been!

So, I met with him and taught him about ACE; how important it is for him to get better in these areas, and how he needs to develop it further.

About a week after our initial session, he lost a mentor suddenly, again to cancer, who had been like a father figure to him.

A significant mark of a "strong" athlete is the ability to bounce back from the things one cannot control. How quick can that rebound be? What is the impact to an athlete, to their team, if they could be back on form in weeks? What about days? Hours? Seconds…?

This athlete, though he has gone through enormous setbacks at such a prime age, because he has a vivid and clear understanding of what truly is in his individual "control," the positive results and his rebound from life's adversities are immediate. I certainly wouldn't bet against him!

To me, ACE is one of the most foundational principles to teach—so much of performance comes back to the elements of it, back to this whole control game.

With the ACE method, I train individuals to place their focus on the only three things they really *can* control so that their focus is unwavering and unbreakable. They choose their attitude; they don't let the circumstances choose it for them. When the storm hits, they don't panic—they spring into action. They do this using specific techniques and tools that I teach them, and that I'll show you in this book.

Imagine if you could do this in your life. If you could really forget about the external things that you're trying to control, those other people, those outcomes. How much energy would you get back to put into yourself? How far could you run if you let yourself off that leash? What incredible things might you be able to achieve?

So often we look at high achievers around us and say, *I wish I could do that.* We tell ourselves that others have some advantage we don't. The ACE method shows that we are all in the same boat. Achieving your potential is a skill, it's something you can learn and get better at.

Imagine the exhilaration of knowing you are in control of the most critical factors of your success—and that they're all you. You have the ability, right now, to unlock that potential and see where it takes you.

Can it really be that simple? Does this really work?

Listen.

I've been an athlete my whole life. I've had the unique privilege to call myself a collegiate athlete (NCAA Division II). I've coached at the youth level, at the high school level, and at the college level. I've worked with professionals, Olympians, and Paralympians, as well as elite soldiers, and I've built from scratch a custom program to develop the next generation of elite warriors.

I've trained thousands of athletes, and even more non-athletes, from all walks of life, all cultures, and religions. I've seen my teaching method transform careers, people, lives. It works, and it keeps working.

No matter your background, interests, sport, or stature—I've probably been there, as an athlete or as a coach.

My job, the way I view it, is to connect with people and help improve their performance. In coaching, connecting with people and establishing trust is a crucial skill—the most crucial skill a coach can have. So when I work with someone, I really get to know them, and when they experience change, I can see it written on their face and feel it in their heart.

I know people tend to be skeptical of the self-help coaching industry at large. Part of that skepticism comes from a feeling of being uncomfortable with looking for help at all, while the other part is largely related to the uncomfortable truth of "I need to change".

In schools, for example, there's a guidance counselor, and they're always offering their help and expertise, letting students and faculty know they're there to listen. But how many times do you see anyone actually go to the guidance counselor's office? Typically, rarely. And if someone does finally pluck up the courage to go, their friends may laugh at them due to the stigma that "something may be wrong with them."

When I'm brought in to talk to someone, and I introduce myself as a mental conditioning coach (MC), I can sense their immediate discomfort, that maybe this is an odd situation, and they're feeling weird about talking to me.

That bothers me. That guidance counselor, that MC, that therapist—they have so much training and knowledge. They have all these tools and resources that they can use to help anyone, even a straight A student—of all people—who may just have test/exam anxiety, or who may be experiencing pressure to do great academically through their advanced placement (AP) classes. The guidance counselor is equipped and prepared for so many common and uncommon situations that you might be experiencing. Yet there's a stigma around talking to someone because you're admitting there's "something wrong."

But the truth is, as a mentor of mine, Trevor Moawad, famously says, ***"You don't have to be sick to get better."*** There doesn't have to be anything wrong with who you are or what you're doing, for you to look for opportunities to improve.

If you've never heard of a "mental conditioning coach" before, that term might sound a bit odd. Just as you have coaches who focus on physical training, some coaches focus on the mental component of sports performance. We help athletes develop confidence and concentration, and practice techniques for executing what they need to do in the moment to stay process-focused in all aspects of performance. All the while, we are helping all performers develop high performance habits.

Each of us is born with these raw skills; we each have our own idea of what makes us confident, the best ways to focus, mostly just following our own instincts. But an MC knows how to take those skills to the next level, to make someone who is at the top of their game, like a high-performing athlete, even better.

My MC practice is grounded in a teaching method I learned years ago that helps people more than almost anything else I've seen: the ACE method.

In this book, I will teach you how to focus on three simple things, improving each one bit by bit and expanding this method into new areas of your life until you gain better control in these in any situation.

A LITTLE ABOUT THE ORIGIN OF ACE

I got my start in the field of Mental Conditioning in the fall of 2011 on the campus of IMG Academy in Bradenton, Florida as an MC intern. The internship program trains the coach how to communicate and connect with athletes to help them perform more confidently and consistently focusing on different aspects of sport performance such as:

» mental toughness
» awareness
» energy management
» thought management and
» teamwork.

I first heard about ACE from Dr. Angus Mugford, the former director of Mental Conditioning Director of IMG (now the Director of high performance with the Toronto Blue Jays), one day when he was teaching a session for tennis athletes on the importance of mentally and physically resetting after every point. He shared that there are only a few things within your realm of control as an athlete, and when you're at your best you can have these three things naturally with little to no energy:

» A Great and Resilient Attitude,
» Un-shakable Concentration, and
» Consistent and Maximum Effort.

Listening to Dr. Mugford explain this concept, I couldn't believe the simplicity of what he shared. I wrote it down but didn't think much of it at the time. Over the weeks and months after that, however, the idea stuck with me. *Three things you can control.* Looking at the athletes and some fellow interns around me, I started to see that a lot of their problem areas and pain points came down to one if not all three of those things. Ever since then I've made ACE a strong foundation of my teaching philosophy.

The ACE concept was initially developed in the late 1990s by two of the original creators of the IMG Mental Conditioning program: Jeff Troesch and Chad Bohling. Since departing their positions with IMG, Jeff has worked with the NBA, MLB, countless Olympians and pros, while Chad has primarily been with the New York Yankees as well as numerous professional athletes and Olympians in different disciplines. Jeff and Chad have also published articles and audio recordings on the ACE concept in 2000, with one reference that is still able to be found through a Google search in Nick Bollettieri's Tennis Handbook (1999).

Although Jeff and Chad were writing about this concept in 1999 and 2000, to my knowledge I have been teaching and reinforcing the ACE method in a very unique manner. With their permission, I've been able to impact so many lives through teaching ACE, so I want to thank them both for their original creation of this concept. Chad has been a terrific mentor to me over the past 5 years, supporting me professionally by letting me, from time to time, bounce ideas off of him and ask for his direction and guidance.

My firm belief in the ACE method comes not only from their teachings but my own personal applications. I've seen how this method works in my own life and the lives of people close to me. This method has changed my perspective on how I handle uncontrollable situations. Instead of reacting impulsively and emotionally, I first dial directly into my attitude, my concentration, and my effort.

In counseling, there are a variety of "grounding techniques" that are used to bring an individual back to the present moment. As athletes, how important is it for us to stay connected to the present moment? It's something we train for all the time. The ACE method takes that practice to the next level, helping us stay connected in the moment, stay positive, and choose how to respond to events rather than reacting to them. This simple method can be applied to every area of your life to provide a guiding principle for those situations that feel entirely uncontrollable.

I know, because I've lived it for the past 8 years.

ABOUT THIS BOOK

For this book to have its full impact, it is vital that you follow some ground rules. These are the same ground rules I've used to train thousands of individuals including youth, amateur, collegiate, and professional athletes, Olympians, wounded warrior veteran groups, and Navy SPECWAR scouts and recruits.

THE GROUND RULES:

1. Be prepared to re-evaluate old habits and assumptions.
2. Don't be afraid to disagree. Critical thinking is an important part of this process.
3. Be determined, patient and consistent; it may take time to see results once you start applying these concepts.
4. Maintain an open, teachable mind.

Now that we are clear on the ground rules, you should know that the order of chapters is intentional. Another foundation of my teaching philosophy is EARS:

Education: learning about a skill/concept/construct that you can use and practice.

Application: applying a skill/concept/construct in your life

Reinforcement: how do you reinforce this skill/concept/construct even when it's not convenient

Support: ongoing support channels such as a coach, a parent, or a teammate to help keep you zeroed, focused, and locked in when we have moments where we struggle and encounter adversity.

This teaching philosophy is borne from how our brains work. Most people assume that learning takes place when you're directly studying it, and when you practice that lesson later, that's just reinforcement. The truth is, we retain information better when we practice it; practice is a crucial aspect of learning. No one knows this better than athletes. So those latter two steps, reinforcement and support, are necessary follow-through to make sure these concepts are embedded in your mind and life.

I have taught ACE many times over, and I must warn you now, I do encounter fierce resistance at times. It can be challenging to be told that there are things outside of your control.

But stick with it, as once you accept the things that you can't control, you can focus on what you can. You will no longer be shocked or dismayed by your failures; missing the shot or underperforming. You don't get distracted by an emotional response to your mistakes, because your focus never shifts from the things that are under your control.

If you are already experiencing some resistance to the ideas I'm presenting, I want you to know that is an excellent sign. It means you stand to gain a lot from this book. The people who fight me on this method the most, are the ones that see the most significant transformation when they consciously decide to commit and use it.

If you follow the rules and read this book in the intentional order, you will learn a lot!

ONE
UNDER THE INFLUENCE PART I
THE CULTURE AT LARGE

THE GROUND RULES:

1. Be prepared to re-evaluate old habits and assumptions.
2. Don't be afraid to disagree. Critical thinking is an important part of this process.
3. Be determined, patient and consistent; it may take time to see results once you start applying these concepts.
4. Maintain an open, teachable mind.

Today's young athletes are up against enormous industry and cultural challenges. These challenges are the basis of my work because I need to know what ideas and practices have become standard for my athletes, in case I need to disrupt some of their thinking. Much of this is also applicable to adults. Consider this an opportunity to view your own "normal" from an outside perspective, and possibly decide to hit the "reset" button.

When your goal is to be a high-performing individual, you need to become aware of your cultural influences, because they shape your potential. As I explained in the previous chapter, not everything that our culture embraces is helpful or useful. We need to consciously choose the things that make us better people and better performers, and be aware of the things that we are drawn to that may not be supporting us as we work to be the best we can be.

The reason this level of care and consciousness is necessary that we are each immersed in a particular cultural environment that is continually giving us behavioral cues and normalizing specific ideas and values.

These cues and values may be positive, or they may be negative, but the important thing is that they are a significant influence on who we are and how we approach situations. If you're going to take control of yourself, you need to evaluate and manage these influences like anything else that affects you.

It's like alcohol or any other mind-altering substance. When you have a few drinks, you don't change into another person, but you do lose a certain amount of control. You're definitely not going to be thinking or performing at your best. Now, we all understand that alcohol affects people this way, so as adults, and especially as athletes, we are careful about how much alcohol we consume and under what circumstances. But we don't always have that same awareness about the mindset underneath our behaviors and our choices.

I will identify some of the practices and ideas that I run into a lot as a coach that affect my athletes' performance, much like one of these substances. What makes many of these practices so dangerous is that to the individual, they may seem normal. It takes someone else to say, "I see this behavior a lot, and it's not good for you."

Think of the process of reading this book as similar to holding on to a rope that I'm pulling. As long as you hold on, you'll get pulled wherever I take you. But imagine if you're holding on to the rope and I'm standing behind you, pushing the rope forward. Where are we going? *Nowhere.*

In other words, I can't make you do anything you don't want to do, and that's not what this process is about. At some points in this chapter, there may be concepts that you don't really connect with. Those would be the points where you let go of the rope. But that rope is long, and it's always beside you, and when a concept comes by that you do connect with, you can grab on to this rope and hang on.

All you need is one concept that you can grab onto, that will change your life. This way, you never get lost, and you never get pulled in a direction that you don't believe in. At the same time, you're the one who has to move; I can't move you.

SOCIAL MEDIA AND DELUSIONS OF GRANDEUR

Before social media, young athletes used to go through a ritual known as "meeting coaches face to face." If you wanted to get any traction at all, you physically needed a coach to come and see you play. You had to look up the coaches you wanted to work with and reach out to them with a phone call or maybe an email. You would go to their camps, meet them and talk to them.

If you couldn't cut it, this is the time when you'd start encountering rejection. You might ask coaches to come to see you, and they wouldn't. Or a coach might come to see you, but then not make an offer. You might have a conversation with a coach or scout, and they might give you some negative feedback. You might go to a camp and see for yourself that you weren't one of the top performers.

At that point, reality would set in, and you would re-evaluate. You'd say to yourself, *maybe instead of chasing 15 AAU tournaments, I'll just do one or two because I might not be a star, but I enjoy playing the game. Maybe I want to be a coach or sports therapist or commentator, so I can still work with this sport that I love, but perhaps not as an athlete.* Or maybe you would eventually move on to a new career in another industry altogether.

If you had a low GPA and you were telling yourself it didn't matter because you were going to get an offer, you would definitely have to re-evaluate and would probably try to get your grades up. Even if you did decide to push through and keep trying, you would do so with the full knowledge that expert opinion was against you. You would know it was a long shot.

But today, those hard at work promoting themselves on social media don't necessarily get that same wake-up call. When haven't had any coaches come to see them their belief may be that it means the coaches just haven't watched their videos. No offers have come in, "Okay, I just need that one video to go viral… then the offers are going to flow!"

All of those views, likes and follows, those online fans, can feed an athlete's ego and keep their dream alive long past its expiration date.

FAKE CONTENT, REAL CONSEQUENCES

As they say, *the internet never forgets*. If you're an athlete on social media, I caution you to be aware of how your social media profile will look to people who are evaluating you professionally. Not just coaches, but university recruiters, and future hiring managers. Many HR professionals look up a candidate's social media before hiring them, to see what kinds of things they're "liking" or participating in, and they avoid candidates who are posting inappropriate content. We see the consequences of this all the time, with celebrities who have old tweets and old photos dredged up and used against them.

It's not a good strategy for an aspiring athlete to try for viral or "edgelord" status, where you're posting content that is shocking, over the top, or advocating for extreme views that you don't really hold, just for attention.

As a young person, your online persona can feel like just a character that you play for laughs, but professionals will take that as a measure of your real character.

I've heard college coaches say that a large social media footprint can be seen as a sign of attention-seeking behavior. All things being equal, many coaches I've spoken with over the years would prefer an athlete with a smaller and more restrained social media presence over someone who has more followers and who might be more inflammatory or controversial.

TRYING TO MEASURE UP IN A PERFECT WORLD

Maybe you're not trying to go viral yourself, you're just viewing other people's content on social media. This can still profoundly impact your self-esteem as a young person. Social media only shows us at our best; we curate the content that we post. We post photos from our date night with our significant other, yet we don't post anything about the argument that we had that morning. And in so doing, we reinforce a habit in ourselves of focusing on what other people will think, and of posting only what we know others will like.

All of this places too much emphasis on what others will see and think about your life. For example, you may post a photo of your date night with your significant other to commemorate that night and cement your feeling that your relationship is strong. But the external approval and validation that you get through social media can become such a strong focus that you no longer feel your life is good enough unless others think it is. You know you've reached that point when you post a photo of your date night *just* so that others will like it, which shows you that your relationship is doing well.

Much like our content, curated and angled to show off the best moments of our lives, we also develop a superficially extended social network online. We build up followers and subscribers instead of friendships. That's not to say that your follower might not be a real friend—they might be—but focusing on gaining Facebook friends for the sake of it is pointless. You couldn't call those hundreds or thousands of Facebook friends if you needed help or if you wanted to talk. They are mostly shallow acquaintances.

As opposed to these "Barbie friendships," I like to teach the "Rule of Eight." It's based on the idea that as human beings we can only maintain about eight meaningful relationships, either with people or with groups of people, at a time.

With social media "friendships" or followers, it's easy to get caught up in bigger numbers than eight. You can become fixated on having hundreds of followers, dozens of notifications, "follows," and "mentions." It's easy to give those things more meaning than they deserve.

This can also have consequences for your real friendships: you "like" something, or you don't "like" something or you "follow" someone, or you don't "follow" them—and it offends someone. Now your friendship with them is strained.

This is not to say there aren't positive aspects of social media. Many people who might have felt alone in their small towns or social circles are now able to find whole communities that share their interests; they can build meaningful friendships and find support. That's great. But the question I would prompt anyone to ask themselves when using social media is, *what am I getting out of this? What is the purpose of this, for me?*

As we all know, social media can become an addiction. It can provide a platform for people to pursue fame and attention. It can create a cycle where you receive positive feedback, which motivates you to post more content, generating more feedback. The more attention you receive, the more emotionally dependent you are on that attention. This cycle can turn ordinary people into narcissists.

In real life, this behavior is sometimes described as "high arrogance, low self-esteem." This refers to kids who act like they're bulletproof, but if something unfavorable happens to them, they collapse. They have no coping mechanisms for any kind of adversity.

MODERN DAY BULLYING

The narcissism that social media tends to foster in people, combined with the fact that it's easy to stay anonymous, has led to an increase in bullying. This new bullying is not like what we used to experience in the playground.

If you were bullied in the '90s or earlier, it mostly happened in public spaces like the schoolyard or even on a bus. You might have been beaten up, had mean things said to you (or about you), but your bully always ran a risk of getting caught. And they could typically only get to you at school, not in your home.

Today, you can get trolled by someone acting anonymously, who, in real life, acts as your friend. We've always had gossip, but real-life gossip came at a risk. You might be overheard, or caught, or confronted. Online trolls have minimal chance of being caught; if you want to hide your identity, you can.

Worst of all, the bullying never stops. When you leave school and you get home, your social media feeds can end up full of people spewing hate at you on every social media profile and platform you have.

Many of us are attracted to social media because we want positive attention from others, but social media has a dark side, too. It can flood you with negative attention and hatred and can push young people to the depths of despair with ruthless effectiveness.

Part of the danger of online bullying is how invisible it can be to the adults in your life. Before the internet, getting bullied often meant getting physically beaten up. Most parents would notice a black eye or a nasty set of bruises, and ask about it to start conversations with you about how to handle it. Today, many parents have no idea about the bullying their kids are facing until something terrible happens. So you don't get those conversations or that support. You don't get to work through incidents of bullying in a way that makes you stronger or more resilient; instead, you just get flooded with negativity until you can't handle it anymore.

For athletes, in particular, social media can be really vicious. For example, imagine a field kicker missing the game-winning kick in a college football game. The fans will be all over that on social media. In an instant, there's nothing but hate being spewed on all social media platforms, through email and any other channels the trolls can find, all directed at an 18-year-old. Or maybe the fan-base at the other school creates a "support hate group," because they're thrilled that the kid missed that field goal.

I've heard Russel Wilson, the quarterback for the Seahawks, say that he stays off ESPN altogether during the season. He doesn't care what people are saying about him; he wants to focus on what the team is doing and what he's bringing to the table. I think that's brilliant.

We live in a knee-jerk society now, where every opinion and fleeting thought can be shared instantly and consequence-free.

Alex Velluto joked in his standup routine on Dry Bar Comedy that the hate you see online is like the new version of the '90s bathroom stall. If you use the washroom in a convenience store or university campus, you can still see the scribbled writing on the walls and doors of the stalls: Hey, call this number for a good time. Hey, John ruined my life. Or hey, Mary is a B-word, and call her for a good time. It was the original anonymous forum, where you could trash talk anyone you wanted. But there was a limited reach for that kind of content, and everyone knew not to take it too seriously.

Now, as Alex Velluto points out with social media, you can broadcast these messages far and wide, *and* you can directly target that person and spam their inbox and Twitter Mentions and comments. All while staying anonymous yourself.

When it comes to learning resilience, you need to develop coping mechanisms, but you can only do that if you encounter manageable levels of bullying or negativity, such that you can overcome and learn from it. It's a case of needing to walk before you run.

For this to happen, you need to experience these negative interactions in an environment where you still have friends, parents, and teachers looking out for you. You should be able to get back up, find support, and experience learning and strengthening.

Instead, online bullying is ongoing and everywhere, and it can leave you isolated and flooded with shame and fear. You need to equip yourself with the tools necessary to navigate the world of the internet and social media, to try and make it as safe as possible for yourself. But you also have to consider that you live in the real world, too, and you need to learn to navigate there, too.

Be aware that social media is also a huge time suck—smartphone addiction is a real thing. A Nielsen study from 2010 found that the average 13–17-year-old sends, on average, 3,339 text messages a month. Girls send an average of 4,050, while boys send 2,539 on average a month. That breaks down to 135 texts per day for girls and 85 per day for boys! Think about how much time out of your day it would take to send 135 texts. If that was 2010, how much time do you reckon the average person spends on socials now?

In the same way that our social content is curated, with only selected moments shown, parts of our lives taken out of context, so too has all media changed. Reality TV shows, for example, have a cynical edge to them; the slogan of Survivor is "Outwit, Outplay, Outlast." It suggests this really fierce, no-holds-barred fight for, well, survival. We see the contestants choosing personas for themselves: "the jerk" or "the nice girl." We see them manipulating others to try to get ahead. It's become a cliché that the romance-based reality shows, like Bachelor, are dominated by the contestants willing to be controversial or inappropriate to help get ratings.

These shows aren't reality; they're scripted and curated and exaggerated. But people love them because they're entertaining, the narratives are easy to follow, and there's always someone to root for and someone to hate.

Our idea of reality has become really skewed over time. There's the reality that we live, and the "reality" of the media. When you start to believe that the world you are seeing on social media and on TV is real, it's only natural to compare yourself to this un-real 'reality'— and that is where your life will become very tough.

Think about your local town election as opposed to the national level. Your local mayor or city counselor tends to run on real issues that affect you: roads that need repairing, which neighborhoods are and aren't being taxed fairly, how small businesses are doing. They may or may not connect themselves to a political party, but the issues are always local, and their stance is to do something that will help people with their real situations, right now. Compare that to the national elections, and it's a very different picture.

Local politics is the reality we actually live in—people we know, circumstances that affect us, that we understand and control. National politics is the "reality" on reality shows and on social media, it's completely incongruent. It's partisan and sensationalized, to the point where it's hard to know what to believe.

This whole book advocates for us to place our focus on the things we can control, the things we can understand and change, things internal to us. But if our attention is being pulled to outside issues, issues that don't relate to us and aren't necessarily relevant to us, we can lose sight of the things that matter.

CELEBRITY CULTURE

What we concentrate on creates our attitude, and our attitude shapes our effort. The online world is full of distractions, attempting to pull our focus so we will spend money or behave a certain way. A huge source of these distractions is celebrity culture. Celebrities are built up to be these stars where every move they make is newsworthy, but a lot of what they do isn't helping anyone or making a difference.

Celebrities can also be poor role models when it comes to discipline. Discipline is such an essential trait for you as an athlete, but the actors and musicians that tend to be the trendiest celebrities are the ones who from this outsider's perspective have the least discipline.

There always seems to be some new scandal in the tabloids that comes back to celebrities and their poor judgment. Some of the more famous examples are Michael Jackson dangling his infant son out a hotel window in Berlin in 2002, Brittany Spears' 24-hour marriage, Miley Cyrus twerking on stage at the MTV VMAs. Then there's Kim Kardashian. Enough said.

Clearly, the most notorious celebrity viral moments are not good examples for aspiring athletes—or really, anyone else. They don't embody traits like discipline, inner strength, or perseverance.

Celebrity culture builds people up, puts them on unrealistic pedestals, and then tears them down by putting their failures all over the news and internet. It's not healthy for the people caught up in it, and it's not healthy for us as consumers, either.

As an athlete, and as a person, you have to be careful where you place your trust and your interest. You may be a fan of a particular actress, and think, *Oh, I just care about her work, her movies. I don't care about her personal life.* But if you're consuming that content, it is entering your mind and being normalized, even if only at a subconscious level. Be deliberate about the content you consume, don't just scroll gossip sites, but focus instead on publications and websites that you know have good-quality content.

MUSIC

Music can be even more of an influence than celebrity culture. We're not always even aware of what we're consuming when we listen to music.

Sometimes, when I encounter an athlete that seems to have a particularly toxic view of the world, I'll ask what kind of music they listen to, just as part of getting to know them. Whatever artists they name, I'll listen to one of their songs and ask some questions:

» Do you agree with everything in the message of this music?
» Does your family/friends/teammates listen to this music?
» Why do you enjoy it?

Often, in these conversations, the athlete will say something like, "I love the beat," or "I love this artist's story." Well, that's great, but what are the lyrics really saying? What does it really mean, what are you really listening to and feeding yourself? Often, they'll tell me what the artist has said about the meaning of the song. Okay, but what does the song mean to you? We'll take apart the lyrics. If you agree morally and ethically with everything the artist is saying, then keep listening to it.

The truth is, our minds absorb everything in the content we consume. Not just the parts that we like or agree with—everything. Some parts speak to our conscious mind and some to our subconscious. And we can be programmed to think and feel certain ways by the content that we pay the most attention to. Most of us may not think very critically about the material we're absorbing, but once you get to the level of an elite athlete, anything you consume can influence your performance. You must manage those inputs just like anything else that goes into your body or your mind.

I had this conversation with one athlete, Steve. I asked him how many hours a day he was listening to his Spotify account. He pulled it up on his phone—4.5 hours day. I said to him, "Steve, you have a toxic worldview, and everything you think about is negative. You can't even take criticism from your coach positively, can you?" He gave me a stone-cold poker face, but he knew he was caught. We worked out a plan to cut out music entirely for two weeks, just to see what would happen. I told him, "Come back to me in two weeks and tell me how you feel." At the end of two weeks, Steve came to me and said, "I don't know how to describe this, but I just feel clean."

VIDEO GAMES

When Grand Theft Auto (GTA) first came out, suddenly people I knew were calling each other by their characters' names from the video game. GTA allows you to play out every kind of criminal and violent behavior you can imagine. Things you would never do in real life, you now have this virtual freedom to act out online—free of any real-world punishment or accountability.

In the game…how fast can you drive your car away from the cops? How quick can you make the drug deal without getting shot at? Want to go steal that guy's motorbike and beat him up because he cut you off in traffic? Be my guest.

That's not harmless nor insignificant. The rewards system in the game feeds into our dopamine drives, it feels good, so we want to spend more time on it and engage with it more.

When I work with young athletes, I teach them that not everything that feels good is good for them. This is sometimes met with resistance. People feel like they are in control of it. They'll tell me, "Just because I play Grand Theft Auto doesn't mean I'm going to go rob a bank." Maybe not, but if I hear you referring to your significant other using some derogatory slang that you don't even believe in, I have to ask: where did you pick that up?

Ultimately, at this point, you have a choice. Like that scene from The Matrix where Morpheus offers Neo the two pills, you can decide whether to take the blue pill or the red pill. If you want to keep doing what you're doing, take the blue pill and go back to your everyday life. Shut this book, because you're not going to like what's coming. But if you're willing to unplug from your music and newsfeeds, and see how great life can be, and reach your full potential, take the red pill. Keep reading.

THE GROUND RULES:

1. Be prepared to re-evaluate old habits and assumptions.
2. Don't be afraid to disagree. Critical thinking is an important part of this process.
3. Be determined, patient and consistent; it may take time to see results once you start applying these concepts.
4. Maintain an open, teachable mind.

TWO
UNDER THE INFLUENCE PART II

THE SPORTS INDUSTRY

THE GROUND RULES:

1. Be prepared to re-evaluate old habits and assumptions.
2. Don't be afraid to disagree. Critical thinking is an important part of this process.
3. It may take time to see results once you start applying these concepts.
4. Maintain an open, teachable mind.

You are working to build your life and your career within a specific cultural environment. That environment has a significant influence on you, just as a natural environment influences the trees that grow there. If you have an environment with fertile soil, lots of rain and sun, you'll see tall, healthy trees. If you have an environment like a desert, no trees can grow at all.

Imagine a bonsai tree. It grows in a pot and is carefully tended to and pruned, to give it a specific shape.

So my question to you young athletes is this. What kind of cultural environment are you growing up in? How has it formed your habits and assumptions?

CULTURE CREATES WORK ETHIC

In this chapter, I'll describe the type of work ethic and focus that an athlete needs to be successful, as well as some mentalities that are not as helpful.

The reason I continue to use and evolve the ACE method, and why it leads to such transformational change for the people who practice it, is because it's so different from the ideas that we absorb from culture at large. The society that we live in plays a huge part in how we see the world and ourselves. It conditions us to expect specific outcomes, make certain choices, question some messages and accept others. It shapes our idea of what "normal" is. We need to be aware of this really significant influence and make a deliberate choice about how, and whether, to engage with or consume it.

THE DANGER OF DELUSIONS OF GRANDEUR

In Hollywood, we continuously see the underdog being celebrated— and that's important, because underdog stories do happen, and they *are* worthwhile stories to tell. However, focusing only on the underdog can send a message to young athletes that anyone can be an elite athlete—regardless of physical characteristics, regardless of training. Some can, it's true—but most won't.

Instead, underdog stories train young athletes to believe that they are each an underdog, and that even if they haven't seen any success yet, they will—as long as they just keep trying.

You might be wondering, *What's wrong with that?* There's nothing wrong with perseverance, but some athletes will develop delusions of grandeur. They might believe, with little evidence, that they are a star athlete in the making, and these athletes may ignore any professional advice they receive that contradicts that. This will not help these athletes. Think about if this may apply to you.

As a coach working at elite sports academies, I saw young athletes who haven't been recruited by any Division 1 or Division 2 schools, with low GPAs, believing they can come to an academy, do a post-grad year, turn it all around and get a Division 1 offer. As though just one year of academy work will make that happen when it hasn't happened yet. What makes it worse is that academy tuition isn't cheap, so I saw some instances of families mortgaging and refinancing their homes to support this vision of "Dream or Bust".

The truth is, many factors in your success as an athlete are outside of your control. Physical characteristics, family income, geographical location, these can all affect an athlete's ability to develop. But the message that our sports industry largely sends to young aspiring athletes is that none of that matters; even their current performance and the interest they've seen so far doesn't matter. The message is that if they keep going, they can *definitely* achieve a full scholarship.

Coaches know how to spot kids that are going to develop into top athletes. Most athletes with potential are getting tracked by coaches by the age of 14 or 15. If someone has reached 17 or 18-years-old without receiving that level of attention, his/her chances of reaching that level of performance decrease exponentially. Of course, it can happen, with late blooming athletes, and athletes who are true diamonds in the ruff, however these cases are extraordinarily rare.

What really happens, in 99 out of 100 cases, is that kid doesn't make it, and it's devastating to them. Their motivation and attitude completely break down. That athlete may have a full-scale identity crisis at the age of 18 because they were absolutely convinced that they were going to be a star athlete at the next level, and when they realize it's not going to happen, their entire world just stops.

Ever heard of the phrase, "Big fish in a small pond"? Do you know how big the oceans of talent really are in the world? It's incredible, and it can be overwhelming for a young athlete to come to that realization if they're not prepared for it.

EXTERNAL SUCCESS VS. INTERNAL STRENGTH

Many of us come to worship certain kinds of people in the public eye; we want to emulate them. However, as an athlete, it's not helpful to focus on the life and career of someone who might be very different from you. The only person who can be just like Kobe Bryant, is Kobe.

Yes, it's important to have role models, but you need to be aware of your unique strengths and limitations to set your own goals accordingly. Your motivation and goals should come from within, from an understanding of who you are and what you believe you can do—not from attempting to recreate someone else's career. Similarly, your strength needs to come from your inner drive and motivation, not an attempt to emulate someone else.

The sports industry at the moment, with its brand endorsements and video games and celebrity athletes, is pulling today's young athletes away from focusing on themselves, the things that are under their control, and the personal work ethic they will need to get there.

Young athletes today are focused on external markers of success rather than the long journey that their favorite athletes took to get there. They believe that they can start from nothing, invest thousands of dollars in going to the right schools and wearing the right brands, and end up exactly where their favorite athletes are—no other requirements. We see "overnight successes" as star athletes become viral, but we never witness the decades of intense work and the sacrifices those athletes made to get there.

The disconnect between what young athletes want and what they believe it will take to get it is growing as the sports industry grows.

INTERNAL VS. EXTERNAL MOTIVATIONS

If you type "motivation" into YouTube, you will find an entire category of beautifully produced, pump-up, motivational videos. They'll feature teams working through a workout or a game, maybe with clips from Rocky, a famous artist or famous author, all about embracing the suck, pushing through the pain, and overcoming failure.

There's nothing wrong with these videos. They show some great stories, and they can be great motivation. They can also be useful on a short-term basis, or on particular occasions like the first game of a season, to inspire and challenge you. I use them in my practice occasionally, but I don't just show a video and stop there. I build on it.

If you just stop there—after viewing the video, you get motivated, go out and do the workout or whatever you need to do—that motivation won't last. You might get a few hours or maybe a few days out of it, but eventually, sooner rather than later, your motivation will run out. What then? Then you just watch another video, and another one.

What's happening here, to use some technical terms, is that you're becoming *dependent on extrinsic motivators*. Your motivation comes from outside factors, these videos, for example, rather than coming from inside yourself.

If you're depending on these motivators and videos, then you're not waking up in the morning, ready for your workout. You need this extra step of watching a video. If it's not a video, maybe it's a song, or a scene from a movie—that scene from Braveheart, with Mel Gibson giving his soldiers a moving speech before they race head on into battle.

But to have a good season, a good game, or even just a good workout, you'll need internal drive. When you're getting bumped and bruised in a game, and you've been hit hard, things haven't gone your way and the whole team is fighting tooth and nail, that motivational video you watched before the game will be long gone from your mind and you'll need to rely on your critical thinking, habits, and your internal fire and drive.

What makes a tough athlete is their ability to get up with an attitude that they set in place a long time ago, prepared to make a choice about how to respond today. Those motivational videos don't capture the blood, sweat, and tears that go into a good season. If you're on a steady diet of extrinsic motivators, chances are you aren't fully prepared for how much work is really needed to perform as an athlete.

To be blunt, my elite athletes and soldiers don't live off watching motivational videos. They don't feel a need to. They've put in the work to get their attitude to the point where they're ready for the workout, or the tough session, or whatever they're up against. Their attitude is rooted in the sense of, *I'm waking up ready to improve, prepared to make decisions that will set the path of my career for the next 10 years. I don't care what obstacles come in my way, I'm ready to conquer.* They don't need to consume this stuff, and they choose not to. They've built the habit of this attitude and embedded it into their mindset.

The work of being an athlete isn't just about getting through one workout, or one game. If it were, everyone would be an elite athlete. As it is, we often never see the "behind the scenes" of elite performance that I just gave you. We see montages, and while we may *know*, intellectually, that a lot of work has gone to create the moments captured in those videos, it's hard to fully understand and appreciate it because we don't see it. Instead, we're motivated based on a reward, an achievement or an objective. Internal drive and motivation are from the heart. It's from the soul. It's from your desire for self-improvement, regardless of the outcome. It's personal. Intrinsic.

If consuming this kind of media and this kind of video is something that you regularly do, that's fine. I just want to inform you that there is a better way. And I want you to keep reading with an open mind.

Keep hanging on, because I'm going to unpack one of the most powerful, impactful predictors of success—much greater than temporary motivation.

Even though what we get to see about celebrity athletes seems so real to us, we have to continually remind ourselves that it, in fact, isn't. In *Wizard of Oz*, when Dorothy reaches the Wizard, she finds out he's a fraud, an image being created by a small man behind a screen. This is much like the internet. While it clearly has real consequences, as a place, it's not real. We create it, and in our efforts to build community, we also create social media platforms which can be really unhealthy and can present a distorted view of the world.

In the same way, we've built up a culture devoting ourselves to a sport, making sacrifices, working through the pain. It can be challenging to put these images into perspective. We see a Nike commercial, and we really believe that this is what every athlete's life looks like, all the time.

BRANDS CREATING DELUSIONS OF GRANDEUR

Materialism is everywhere, it's basically a fact of life at this point. We are very attached to our status symbols, and we invest a lot of significance in the purchases we make, the brands we like, who those brands' spokespeople are. A word of caution to you here—a particular arm brand or pair of compression leggings probably won't make you a better ball player.

Beyond the materialism of brand loyalty, sports brands put out messages about what it means to be an athlete that simply aren't healthy. Messaging along the lines of "Sport is life," commercials focusing on the intensity of the workout, the sacrifices made. It's this grandiose, pseudo-inspirational messaging about giving up everything for your sport that can really give people the wrong message.

It can be really dangerous to focus your whole life on one activity. What about school? Friends? Relaxation and downtime? You should be developing in every area of their life. You need hobbies and interests outside of sport. You need to have situations where you can just be a kid, where you can learn healthy social skills and interact with other kids without having it be about the sport and the competition.

It's not healthy for anyone, even professional athletes, to put the sport first and sacrifice everything else to it. Sports commercials can romanticize those sacrifices—the early practices, the long drives to games, the pain and injuries—but if a real person tries to sacrifice everything in their life for the sport in that same way, two things will happen. First, they'll alienate themselves from their family and friends, because those activities are taking away from time they could be putting into their relationships. Secondly, they're setting themselves up for heartbreak when the time comes that they can't play anymore.

Many athletes sadly are encouraged to base their entire being on sports, to spend all of their time on it, until sports consumes their whole life. These people don't have a solid foundation for their identity. If one day they can't play that sport for whatever reason, or their sports career comes to an end, they'll collapse. It will be tough for them.

When I work with professional athletes, I really encourage them to think about their outside interests. What do you enjoy doing? Do you have a family? If you don't, that's fine, are you into art? Do you like the stock market? Hobbies? You have to have something. That way, if your sport gets taken from you—because you cannot control how long you play your sport—your whole life won't be ruined.

You need to prepare yourself for the fact that your career can end abruptly at any given point, any given time, not of your choosing. In doing so, set yourself up for success and have other things that you can transition into after sports; a foundation for a fulfilling life after your sports career has ended.

If you allow sports to be your life, be prepared to be disappointed. Be prepared for more bad days than good days.

The message I think athletes really need to hear from a sports commercial is a celebrity athlete saying, "Listen. I love my sport. I love being challenged to work hard and be disciplined. I love working with my coaches and my team for something bigger than myself. I love outworking my opponent, bouncing back from a failure, picking myself up after a loss. But by the way, I also have a life. I am a father or mother first. I am a husband or wife. A friend to many. Sports is my arena to compete, but I have a whole life outside of it where I am a human being and part of a larger society."

I would love to see sports commercials where you see an athlete, not in their professional realm with their sports gear and jersey, but waking up at 2AM to feed their baby. I want kids and people to see that sports does not equal life. It's an *enhancer* to life. It brings fulfillment, enjoyment, energy, excitement, but it can't embody life. You must not let it.

Most of what we see in our culture is smoke and mirrors. The motivational videos, the sports commercials, the branding; it's not reality. Those things may seem powerful and inspirational, but they can also be disempowering. They have the potential to take away your natural resilience, your innate ability to focus and concentrate, and instead create distractions, confusion and unrealistic expectations.

I want you to wake up and to be aware of how you are devoting your time, money, energy, and attention to your sport. There's nothing wrong with committing to something and investing in it, but we need to be deliberate about our attitude, and bring our inner strength and drive to the table, rather than allowing external approval or commercialized examples to pull us in any direction.

For most people, this means being humble enough to re-evaluate everything. Most of us don't have the strength to resist these external forces, to never give in. The more common path is to wake up at some point, realize that we've gone in a direction that no longer reflects who we are or where we want to be, and make significant adjustments. It's about being able to consider the possibility that maybe your whole approach up until this point has been wrong.

Ask yourself: Have you ever thought of your sport as something all-encompassing, something to devote your entire life to? Or do you think of it as just one part of your life? Remember the ground rule about being honest and open. Look at yourself in the mirror. Nobody else has to know it except you. But answer that question honestly; take this opportunity to be transparent and have that moment of reckoning with yourself.

THE GROUND RULES:

1. Be prepared to re-evaluate old habits and assumptions.
2. Don't be afraid to disagree. Critical thinking is an important part of this process.
3. Be determined, patient and consistent; it may take time to see results once you start applying these concepts.
4. Maintain an open, teachable mind.

THREE
UNDER THE INFLUENCE PART III

PARENTS AND COACHES

THE GROUND RULES:

1. Be prepared to re-evaluate old habits and assumptions.
2. Don't be afraid to disagree. Critical thinking is an important part of this process.
3. Be determined, patient and consistent; it may take time to see results once you start applying these concepts.
4. Maintain an open, teachable mind.

The last sphere of influence that we need to be aware of as athletes (and as people) are the authority figures in our lives, the people who drive us forward and mentor us. As a coach, I'm seeing a trend of parents and coaches putting too much pressure on youth and preventing them from building resilience and adaptability. Your parents and your coach are some of the most important people in your life, especially when it comes to developing as an athlete, but they're not perfect. It's important to be aware of some of the ways you can be influenced towards unhealthy behaviors.

I love the book, *Inside-Out Coaching* by Joe Ehrmann so much, that I developed the name of my business based on Joe's major elements presented in his book.

If Joe Ehrmann were to summarize what it means to be a "transformational coach" in three sentences, I think it would be this:

"Sports doesn't build character. That's a myth. It's up to us as coaches to demand and coach it."

What he means is, sports can be a vehicle for character development, but it's the coaches and parents who really do the work. You cannot rely on a sport to develop character. If you could, why isn't every young athlete a paragon of discipline and self-control? Why is it that I can watch a youth (and sometimes, adult ones too) tennis tournament and see kids throwing temper tantrums, breaking and throwing rackets?

Why do I see coaches laying into an athlete because they went off the game plan? Why do I see parents visibly upset, walking out of the court, and sitting in their car steaming, frustrated, or emotional while the kid's still playing?

Coaches are responsible to building, instilling, and demanding character. Coaches model character. Look at many successful programs across the country, and listen to how many of those coaches speak of and demand character from their athletes and leaders. The name Mike Krzyzewski, who also goes by "Coach K," may come to mind, or maybe John Wooden, Nick Saban, Muffet McGraw, Pete Carrol, Bill Bellicheck, Pat Summit, Scott Frost, Phil Jackson, or Geno Auriemma...We could go on and on, but look at these instrumental and influential coaches—they're preaching and *demanding* character.

Parents, too, have that same ability to demand, model and coach character.

The whole philosophy of Inside Out Coaching is about how we want to coach from an inside perspective. We want to know the human being *for the human being*. We want to see the individual for the individual.

Joe is teaching the opposite of a transactional approach: *what can that kid do for me?*

In this win-at-all-cost culture that we live in, how do you measure success as a coach? As Joe says, if you're measuring success by the scoreboard, you've lost.

Of course, on some level, winning is important. If you don't win as a coach, you may very well be out of a job. But a coach can win a heart a lot easier than they can win a game because they can't control a game. They can choose the amount of effort to invest in you as an athlete or to learn about your life. They can control the kind of approach they take with athletes, a more interpersonal approach. Not to be a friend—but a mentor to you.

Many coaches have a transactional approach. It's about wins and losses, it's about what that athlete and that team can do for them, it's about status and prestige. It's not about the individual.

Three-Dimensional Coaching (3D-Institute) uses the image of a pyramid. The bottom level of the pyramid is the fundamentals. Those are the physical attributes that you spend most of your time working on with a coach: skills, technique, strength, power, and so on.

The second tier is the mind or psychology of an athlete. It covers things like confidence and team cohesion.

The top tier, the smallest portion of that pyramid, is the heart of the athlete.

Most coaches miss the mark and coach from the bottom of they pyramid up, insted of top down.

Ask yourself what the coaches and mentors in your life are focusing on. Think about these things when you select a team. If your coaches are missing the mark here, then it's crucial for you as the athlete to realize it so that you don't confuse their shortcomings with your own transgressions. And if you are currently, or are looking into becoming, a coach yourself, hold these lessons in your heart so that you can cultivate the best environment for your future athletes.

BULLDOZER PARENTS

You've heard of helicopter parents. They're famous for hovering over a kid and picking them up, rescuing them, saving them. These days, in my line of work, I'm seeing a different kind of parent: bulldozer parents. Parents that just plow through their kids by solving their problems, needs, and wants while leaving them in their wake. Even when intentions may be good, these parents have a devastating effect.

A helicopter parent hovers over their kid to rescue them by pulling them out. That's not ideal because it often means parents will take over what was supposed to be the child's fight, and therefore their win (or loss). But at least they don't leave a path of destruction behind them. Bulldozer parents take things a step further.

The coach, the parents, the support crew, work hard to build up and develop a team or an athlete. But it only takes one bulldozer parent to run it all over, to destroy everything. Then, we are left to patch it all up and put everything together again—all because of one parents' self-importance and obsession with flattening everyone else for the perceived benefit of *their* child. Not only do they not let their children fight their own battles, but they crush other people, leaving an emotional mess behind them.

I believe firmly that you as a young athlete need to experience healthy amounts of adversity. You need to be allowed to navigate emotional situations for yourself.

Playgrounds used to be dangerous, from a modern point of view. They had monkey bars. They had concrete that broke bones and tore skin when you fell down or gravel that could be thrown and you could skin up a knee, elbow, or hands. There was wooden equipment that splintered. Arguments that happened on these playgrounds weren't broken up immediately either.

From the collections of the Dallas History & Archives Division, Dallas Public

On the older playgrounds, as an 8–12-year-old kid, you needed some self-sufficiency. You needed to know how to avoid the different ways of getting hurt; how to be careful not to fall when climbing over concrete; how to try not to run on gravel because you'd slip and skin your knee. You needed some fundamental interpersonal skills too: you needed to be able to address whatever grievances or issues might come up with you and your friends.

Did you know that now, in some school districts across the United States that monkey bars are banned from playgrounds? The concrete has largely been replaced with wood chippings or rubber tire mulch. The equipment is ultra-safe, with no drops, or edges, and certainly no splinters. You no longer have the opportunity to learn the same lessons through adventure and play.

"DO YOU KNOW HOW MUCH THIS COSTS?"

A parent who shouts in earshot of their athlete, or even directly to their athlete, "Do you know how much this sport and your training costs?" should really think about the impact of those words. Don't think this happens? Ask some of your friends if they have any experiences such as this. This is happening more and more in our ever-changing landscape of sport.

So many problems come from this type of statement. Here's a few (a far from exhaustive list): bullying/narcissistic behavior from the parent → athlete internalizes their worth to being a price tag → athlete feels devalued → athlete loses and changes motivation(s) → athlete, when playing next, will be worried about not letting parents down (anxiety) instead of playing their sport → the parent has put in jeopardy their relationship on a personal level with their child.

I challenge you to think what kind of positive result will come from these types of hurtful comments? If you an athlete, are on the receiving end of these types of comment, I encourage you to seek help immediately from another adult, perhaps a coach, one of your friend's parents, maybe your school counselor or principal?

These comments are not okay, and I encourage you to be pro-active to seek help in working through these things.

This creates such a disorienting experience from a young person's point of view, as many young athletes flat don't know what things cost. If a young athlete is flying to a camp, they're just excited to go on an airplane. They don't know it's a $500 plane ticket. It's not fair to yank someone out of that childlike excitement when they're not equipped to think about money and costs. It's wrong for an athlete to feel guilty over something they may not be capable of understanding.

Young people are also generally not in control of the financial decisions of the household—it's the parent's choice to spend money on their child's training, so it doesn't make sense to take it out on their kid, who is effectively helpless, when the parent gets stressed.

Worst of all, it treats that child as a means to an end. The message it screams is that your sport and you my son/daughter are purely transactional—the parent's point is, "I'm investing *this* much money into you, the least you can do is show up and have a good smile on your face, even though you lost badly in this tournament. Because I paid 10 grand for you this year."

You can see how this enables parents to use money to bully their kid out of their normal emotional reaction. Now the young athlete doesn't get to have a bad day or work through a hard loss because they have to put on a brave face all the time, or they'll seem ungrateful.

Ask yourself: has your parent ever said to you, "Do you know how much money this costs?" If so, that should be an immediate red flag. Any family where this has happened should have a direct conversation about rethinking their values and priorities, or please seek immediate counseling support from a professional who can help set and manage healthy expectations and limits for unhealthy parent/athlete relationships.

There is another kind of parenting that is also harmful, and that you need to look out for in your own authority figures: helicopter parents. These aren't as detrimental as bulldozer parents, but still not ideal. There is a trend towards bubble-wrapping kids and trying to protect them from any kind of disappointment or failure. Parents dive in to save them from the slightest mishap, praise them when they haven't earned it, and attack others in the name of protecting their own.

A favorite author and speaker of mine, Dr. Tim Elmore, wrote an article called *Three Huge Mistakes We Make Leading Kids and How to Correct Them*. These are the mistakes he lists:

» We Risk Too Little. Why? We fear for their safety.
» We Rescue Too Quickly. Why? We fear for their status.
» We Rave Too Easily. Why? We fear for their self-esteem.

This is a fantastic article about modern parenting culture. I highly recommend you go read it and show it to your parents.

In sports, this looks something like the following:

"Johnny, guess what? You made four for four on your free throws. Let's go get you that new pair of Jordans."

Instead, it's better to believe that doing something well is its own reward, that certain tasks like helping out around the house, are just a basic expectation and not something you get rewarded for doing. This is "intrinsic drive," or the motivation to complete a task because it's inherently satisfying to you, not because of external pressure or reward.

In my line of work, transactional parenting is rife, with kids expecting rewards just for meeting basic expectations.

As a response to this, the trophy industry has boomed in the past ten years. Twenty years ago when you participated in something, *sometimes* you'd get a ribbon. Now, when you participate in recreational sports, you get a trophy—*Hey Johnny, you got ninth out of ninth in this foot race. Thanks for coming, enjoy this twelve-inch-tall participation trophy.*

I'm planning to put my son in youth sports once he becomes of age, to get him active and learning about sports and how to be a team player. My wife and I have already been talking about local soccer leagues that we might be interested in having our son play in when the time comes. I know of a national organization that does a lot of good work, but they happen to have a practice of giving participation medals. All athletes who participate in this organization receive medals at the conclusion of the season, regardless whether they win or lose. "Everyone is a winner!"

Tell me, what aspect of real life does this mantra exist—that everyone is a winner?

When my son is old enough, we'll talk to him and we will teach him about winning and losing. We'll explain to him that you can enjoy your wins, and learn from your losses, but there is a difference between the two. You don't get the same reward (trophy / medal) for winning as you do for when you lose. Sports is about taking risks and living with the outcomes, not about feeling good no matter what.

Giving your all in anything you do in life is very important, but by being over-rewarded just for participation is harmful. In the real world, you are rewarded for your output, usually, no matter how much you put in. This is a lesson that will come as a massive shock to you if learned too late. You should be putting every effort in because of an internal motivator and drive, not because you are seeking an external reward. This simply does not happen during most of life.

In this book, I'll teach you how to use the ACE method to build your intrinsic drive. I'll help you become more deliberate and purposeful about how you move through life and set goals for yourself.

THE ALLURE OF A FREE COLLEGE RIDE AND PROFESSIONAL FUTURE

Every year, the NCAA updates their statistics on the percentage of athletes who go from high school sports to NCAA teams and sports, as well as the percentage of athletes that go from the collegiate ranks to the pros. The numbers through the years have not changed much, but approximately 3-12% of high school seniors that play on a high school team, across the country, will go on to play a collegiate sport. And from those select athletes who play collegiately even fewer will go on to play professionally. The NCAA states that in four of the major professional sporting markets—men's basketball, women's basketball, football, and men's soccer—you have less than a 2% chance of going pro if you're at a collegiate level. The other two major markets, baseball and men's ice hockey, are at 9.5% and 6.4%, respectively.

	High School Participants	NCAA Participants	Overall % HS to NCAA	% HS to NCAA Division I	% HS to NCAA Division II	% HS to NCAA Division III
MEN						
Baseball	491,790	34,980	7.1%	2.1%	2.2%	2.8%
Basketball	550,305	18,712	3.4%	1.0%	1.0%	1.4%
Cross Country	266,271	14,350	5.4%	1.8%	1.4%	2.2%
Football	1,057,382	73,063	6.9%	2.7%	1.8%	2.4%
Golf	141,466	8,527	6.0%	2.1%	1.7%	2.2%
Ice Hockey	35,210	4,199	11.9%	4.8%	0.6%	6.5%
Lacrosse	111,842	13,899	12.4%	2.9%	2.3%	7.1%
Soccer	450,234	24,986	5.5%	1.3%	1.5%	2.7%
Swimming	138,364	9,691	7.0%	2.7%	1.1%	3.1%
Tennis	158,171	7,957	5.0%	1.6%	1.1%	2.3%
Track & Field	600,136	28,595	4.8%	1.8%	1.2%	1.7%
Volleyball	57,209	2,007	3.5%	0.7%	0.7%	2.0%
Water Polo	21,286	1,013	4.8%	2.7%	0.7%	1.3%
Wrestling	244,804	7,175	2.9%	1.0%	0.8%	1.1%
WOMEN						
Basketball	430,368	16,532	3.8%	1.2%	1.1%	1.5%
Cross Country	226,039	15,966	7.1%	2.6%	1.8%	2.7%
Field Hockey	60,549	6,066	10.0%	3.0%	1.3%	5.7%
Golf	75,605	5,372	7.1%	2.9%	2.1%	2.2%
Ice Hockey	9,599	2,355	24.5%	8.8%	1.2%	14.5%
Lacrosse	93,473	11,752	12.6%	3.7%	2.7%	6.2%
Soccer	388,339	27,638	7.1%	2.4%	1.9%	2.8%
Softball	367,405	19,999	5.4%	1.7%	1.6%	2.1%
Swimming	170,797	12,684	7.4%	3.3%	1.2%	2.9%
Tennis	187,519	8,736	4.7%	1.5%	1.1%	2.1%
Track & Field	494,477	29,907	6.0%	2.7%	1.5%	1.8%
Volleyball	444,779	17,387	3.9%	1.2%	1.1%	1.6%
Water Polo	20,826	1,159	5.6%	3.4%	0.9%	1.3%

	NCAA Participants	Approximate # Draft Eligible	# Draft Picks	# NCAA Drafted	% NCAA to Major Pro	% NCAA to Total Pro
Baseball	34,980	7,773	1,215	735	9.5%	--
M Basketball	18,712	4,158	60	50	1.2%	19.3%
W Basketball	16,532	3,674	36	34	0.9%	4.9%
Football	73,063	16,236	253	253	1.6%	1.9%
M Ice Hockey	4,199	933	217	60	6.4%	--
M Soccer	24,986	5,552	88	78	1.4%	--

Sources: High school figures from the 2016-17 High School Athletics Participation Survey conducted by the National Federation of State High School Associations; data from club teams not included. College numbers from the NCAA 2016-17 Sports Sponsorship and Participation Rates Report.

Last Updated: April 20, 2018

With those numbers stated, it's hard to look past just how difficult it truly is to make it to the professional ranks. I really like the NCAA's statement right above the graphs: "the likelihood of an NCAA athlete earning a college degree is significantly greater; graduation success rates are 86% in Division I, 71% in Division II and 87% in Division III".

That was the logic behind those NCAA commercials years ago, where you would see a girl saying, "I'm an engineer," and then diving off a diving board. Or a football player saying, "I love math, as he turns around from the whiteboard as a teacher" and then putting on his football helmet. The tagline that sticks out from the NCAA commercials from old is, "There are over 400,000 NCAA student-athletes and just about all of us will go pro in something other than sports."

It's rare. The NCAA gets it.

If you are involved in youth sports, you have to understand that the chances of becoming the next Tiger Woods or Brett Favre or LeBron James or Serena Williams are so, so, so slim.

That doesn't mean it can't happen. That doesn't mean that you shouldn't aspire to do that if that's your goal. But make sure that you have a healthy process of trying to get there. Families spend tremendous amounts of time and money convinced that they're going to get a college scholarship at the end of it. Like the mythical pot of gold at the end of the rainbow, it can be an alluring goal that is very tough to reach.

It's not that you shouldn't hope for a scholarship, and work towards that but there are so many things outside of your control. It's dangerous to put that college scholarship as the only end goal, the only measure of success.

ANXIETY IS CREATED FROM NOTHING

The danger of focusing on that scholarship, that offer, that golden ticket, is that it can come with the fear of failure. If you tell yourself that there's only one acceptable outcome, get ready for a lot of hard nights filled with stress and worry.

When an external reward is your only motivation, you become obsessed with the milestones that mark your progress towards that goal. When you hit a marker of success, you're elated, but if you miss one, you're crushed. I see student-athletes worrying: *Well, the college scout isn't calling me back* or, *They didn't see my best games* or, *Nobody's calling me, and it's my senior year—I'm not getting recruited.*

This drive and this allure to play college sports and to get recruited, in some athletes, is so strong throughout their youth and adolescence, it creates an unhealthy, artificial pressure.

When you're under those kinds of pressures, the natural tendency is for your sport to become work. You may have first got involved with the sport because you were naturally gifted, or you loved it and thought it was fun. All of a sudden, with this pressure, the goalpost has shifted. Now, instead of just continuing to play for fun with a goal in mind, it becomes work and stress, and overcoming adversities is more challenging. If it were fun, it would be easier to handle the moments of difficulty because the sport's still fun, and that carries more weight than the adversity.

SPORTS IDOLATRY

Idolatry is an old-fashioned Christian word but hang on while I explain what it means and how it relates to you as an athlete.

If you're not familiar with this word, idolatry means worshipping a physical object like it's God. The Bible has a lot to say about false idols and the people who worship them, and it's never good. Today, Christians apply this concept throughout their lives. They try to stay focused on God and watch out for anything that might pull their focus or distract them, anything that might start to take a place in their heart where God should be.

Do you see how this idea relates to athletes? It's all about choosing to place your focus on the things that are true to you, and lasting, and worthy of your effort and devotion. And maintaining that focus even when other distractions come along.

As an example, one night, I was hanging out with a friend of mine who had just come back from a Nebraska Cornhusker football game. Four hours after the game, he was still so angry and bitter because his team lost. The crowd was in tears—everyone from old men to young kids, crying with tears running down their faces. He shared that he saw real grief and despair and agony in people's faces.

It was really striking to me to hear and see on T.V. that kind of an emotional reaction. Looking back, I realize now that the fans idolized that football team and when that team lost, it was devastating to them. In a way, their "false god, their titan, their hero" was just defeated.

That's a glaring example of idolatry. But this idea is everywhere in our lives—that we should devote ourselves to some external thing, some object. A sports team, a celebrity, a politician.

A buddy of mine, a stockbroker, makes excellent money. He just bought a really sweet Lexus car, a coupe. One night when he was driving, his car gets hit by a garbage truck and is totaled. My friend was incredibly upset because he loved that car. Really loved it. For weeks on end after that wreck when we'd get together for networking functions, all I would hear about was his car and how he can't replace it.

There's nothing wrong with enjoying material objects, but when we start to become so emotionally invested that we actually grieve when we lose them, I think those relationships really need to be re-evaluated. My buddy was so focused on his car, he didn't even stop to think about the fact that he wasn't hurt, that the other driver and his passengers were fine, all these things that are much more important at the end of the day.

Idolatry runs in so many different aspects of our life. It could be a car, a job or a career, or even a spouse, sibling or family member. It can be a sport.

To see if you're idolizing an interest of yours, something you're over-emotionally invested in, just picture that thing and ask yourself: if it was to be taken away from you, if you could never participate or enjoy it again, or if you had no further association with it, how would that feel?

This is a tough thing to think about. Above I even mentioned sensitive matters such as a career, or a close family member. Of course, losing those close to us or a career we've built may feel like it would cause uncontrollable grief, and you're most likely right to feel those things immediately after. I don't want you to think that I'm some heartless dude who is saying disconnect... but in a way, I kind of am. I'm saying losing any of those things should not mean you lose your identity or your reason for being.

To carry on with the Biblical theme, in the Old Testament of the Bible (Job 1:21) there is a phrase we've probably heard many times in our lives. ***The Lord giveth, and the Lord taketh away.*** Think of it... all things that come into our life can bring fulfillment, enjoyment, engagement, disappointment, sadness, despair, etc. You get both sides of the emotional coin, but the end-game that you can put your attention into is a faith of that which is not within your control. You come into the world naked with nothing, and you're going to leave this world naked, not taking any of the material gains with you as well.

People *can* move on after a sudden or tragic loss of family. It may take years—shoot, it may take a lifetime—and that's okay, we all work at our own paces. We can move on from losing a much-loved career. We *can* accept that the Nebraska Cornhusker football team fought in that game, smile and appreciate that we got to watch a great game, and leave the stadium hoping the team can win on the scoreboard next time.

I have a direct challenge for you.

Picture losing one thing that you're really close to.

A position in your sport. A coach who takes another coaching job. A girlfriend who breaks up with you. A boyfriend who breaks up with you. You didn't make the play. If you're a coach, your star player goes down with a season-ending injury. You personally suffer a career-ending injury.

If you pictured losing that thing and you can see the immediate and prolonged grief and despair, I challenge you to re-evaluate your relationship with whatever object or situation it may be. Remember, the purpose of sport is to enhance life. It isn't life itself.

It must not be allowed to be life.

We are all, right now, being taught and trained by our culture to care more about material things, lustful desires, things that our own morals and values don't lead us towards, but we go towards them anyway.

Do your actions, your behaviors, your attitude match who you say you are?

This is a tough question. It puts you on the spot, makes you really confront your image of yourself, how you like to think you are, with how you really are.

How do you get to be someone that you don't want to be? It happens more easily than you think if you're not deliberate about choosing who you are and following through. There are so many cultural influences and deceptions waiting to trap you if you decide to stop putting effort into choosing your character.

Think of a Venus Fly Trap. It lures insects in with its odor, they fly right past all the warning signs. Similarly, athletes can get sucked into the illusions and pressures from the outside world—coaches, the sports industry as a whole, pop culture, family, all these different sources of external pressure. They get sucked in, and their focus is on these external things. They're not growing or developing, not really, because all of their energy is going outside of themselves, reaching for an image that they think will guide them. But it's just leading them to focus on appearances—*Does this jersey make me look like LeBron?*—and not on performance.

We're caring a hell of a lot more about the outcome of our circumstances than the attitude and energy that we're putting into our activities, and where we're investing our time.

We've been talking so far about some of the different challenges of the culture that we live in and how it's manipulating us to be *under the influence of artificial values.*

Next, we're going to talk about the things that really are important and the way to build yourself into being a mentally tough person.

You need to start at the core with a strong foundation.

Here's my promise to you: Hang on. Keep an open mind, keep an empty cup because it's about to get filled. As difficult as some of these things may be to swallow, as much as you may want to push back and fight me, bring that fight to the next chapter because you're going to need it here. I'm going to continue to challenge you and make you think.

THE GROUND RULES:

1. Be prepared to re-evaluate old habits and assumptions.
2. Don't be afraid to disagree. Critical thinking is an important part of this process.
3. Be determined, patient and consistent; it may take time to see results once you start applying these concepts.
4. Maintain an open, teachable mind.

FOUR

CIRCLE OF CONTROL

THE GROUND RULES:

1. Be prepared to re-evaluate old habits and assumptions.
2. Don't be afraid to disagree. Critical thinking is an important part of this process.
3. Be determined, patient and consistent; it may take time to see results once you start applying these concepts.
4. Maintain an open, teachable mind.

We've discussed the cultural environment that today's young athletes are entering, and here's where ACE comes in. ACE is a teaching method and, really, a way of looking at the world in terms of what you **do and don't control**. Most athletes are convinced that they control many factors of their performance, when in fact, there are very few things that an athlete really controls 100% of the time. Be prepared to have your assumptions adjusted in this chapter as I teach you an entirely new way of looking at your performance.

In the activity below, you will be given a word bank with several variables that you encounter in sport. Your job is to place each variable either inside of or outside of the circle of control. If you believe you can control the variable, place it inside the circle. If you believe that you can't control the variable, place it outside of the circle.

INSTRUCTIONS:

Your job as the participant is to place each variable from the word bank below either inside or outside of the Circle of Control.

If you believe that you can control a variable, you need to place it inside the circle. If you believe that you cannot control the variable, you need to place it outside of the circle.

I challenge you to take this activity seriously and to think critically about each variable.

This activity is the first step to being able to not only view any challenge as a growth opportunity, but to embrace it as a growth opportunity.

Because the first step is to understand what is under your control.

Seriously. Do the exercise.

WORD BANK:

outcome • personal performance • teammates • warm-up(s) • attitude • communication • opposing player comments • opposing crowd • percentages • results • referees/umpires • schedule of events • weather • media • facilities • altitude • teammates running correct play • opponent's faster than you • ball too flat/too bouncy • concentration • teammates don't pass the ball • strategy • opponents' strategy • effort • coach's opinion • teamwork • technique

1. **Inside** = things you have control over
2. **Outside** = things that you don't have control over

CIRCLE OF CONTROL

An activity that brings awareness to things that are inside or outside of our "control" when we compete

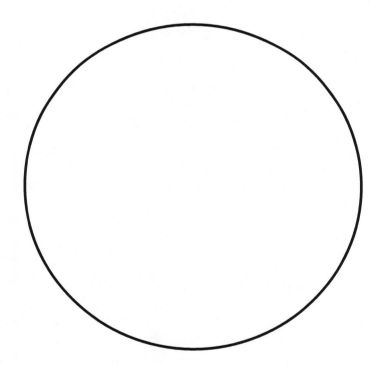

Good work. Now that you have completed the entire word bank can you think of any others to add either inside or outside the circle? If so please add them now.

Now, look at the circle in front of you.

Here is one piece of instruction I left out on purpose. Things that *belong* inside the circle…are things that you have **100%** control of, every single game, every single practice, every single day. And remember…

$$99.99999\% \neq 100\%$$

Does this change any of your answers?

There's a good chance, your circle could look something along the lines of this!

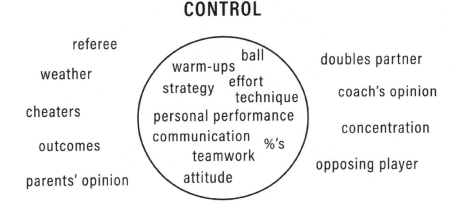

I've done this activity enough to know that you'll have things to move, and I would encourage you to take the time to do so right now.

Thank you for being vulnerable and filling out this exercise. When you pause, take the time to do this, mastery of these skills will come much quicker. You're on a great path. Keep hanging on!

Let's first examine the top 5 most commonly misplaced variables.

COMMUNICATION, WARM-UPS & PERSONAL PERFORMANCE

Have you ever had a bad warmup? Do you believe you're in control of your warmups?

Take a look. Where did you place it—inside or outside of your control? Why? What factors went into your reasoning?

The truth is, everyone has a bad warm up. If you say you haven't, you're lying. See Ground Rule #2: "Be Honest and Open."

Think back: if you don't remember a lousy warmup (which I'm highly skeptical of), maybe there was a time when a coach asked you to execute one skill, or one play, in a game and you messed up. Was that in your control? You were the one playing it, sure, but that doesn't mean it was 100% in your control.

Let's say you misunderstood what he asked, perhaps your coach wasn't clear about what he wanted you to do—now there is miscommunication between you and another party so of course, it's no longer 100% in your control. A minor miscue only has to happen once to have a significant impact on what you do. That's it. The belief system behind this whole principle, this entire book, is getting to the root of what we can actually control, and what we cannot control.

Communication, warm-ups, personal performance. If you put them on the inside of the circle of control, you need to move them out. They don't belong there because you cannot control them 100% of the time.

Don't look at the 99% of the times you managed to take control back—during the 1% where you didn't have full control, what were some of the reasons that you didn't? Was somebody shouting and being a distracting when your coach was talking to you? Did you have a bad warm up because you just were out of sync or perhaps because you were coming down with a cold? There is any number of things that can affect communication, warmups and personal performance, which goes to show how far it is from being under your control.

RESULTS/OUTCOME/PERCENTAGES

One of the biggest traps that athletes get stuck in is believing, on some level, that you can control your outcomes, your results, or your percentages 100% of the time.

Of course, you can't. Not really.

If you accept that, just for now, for the sake of argument—that you can't control your outcomes—does that change your perspective on the emphasis you put on your stats or the results?

It should.

There's nothing wrong with wanting to compete and win. No athlete should be going into a competition wanting to lose. But where are your energy and attention directed? If it's on one of these three things predominantly—results, outcome, percentages—you're walking into a trap before that game's even started.

If your primary focus before the game is on winning, and winning by a lot, and making a certain number of free-throw shots (for example), you're walking into a thinking trap as you enter that arena. Even as a coach.

Because when you're letting those things dictate your thought, as the game progresses, when things don't go according to plan, you suddenly become tight, frustrated, insecure, bitter and angry. Once you're in these thinking traps, Pandora's box opens and any amount of negativity can come out—it's unpredictable and uncontrollable.

This frequently happens when athletes put their attention on things that belong on the outside of the circle.

The ACE method is about defending yourself from that downward spiral, that pit of negativity, by focusing on the things you truly can control 100% of the time.

STRATEGY

Now, I get a lot of pushback at this point from athletes, coaches, and even the military personnel I have worked with. I bet you're thinking, *OK, Trevor. Maybe basketball stars don't control every warmup. But that doesn't apply to me or my situation. I really do control every aspect of what I do.*

I taught an ACE session years ago on this very concept of controllables with a group of NSW Scouts (Navy Special Warfare). This Naval Recruiting Division in Ohio were referred to as: NRD – Ohio NSW Scout Team. While I was working at SPIRE Institute, a US Olympic & Paralympic Training Site, one of them happened to be a Navy SEAL operator. He spoke up with conviction in the session to explain his perspective on why I was wrong about strategy.

"Trevor, listen. With every aspect of our mission, we control everything about it. Every detail, all the training and preparation, the insert, the exit, you know—the operation, it's all 100% in our control. Every aspect of it is controlled."

I replied, "It sounds like you've got all the bases covered. One thing though... You've got plans A, B, and C for each objective and you know your exit strategy, and so on. Right?"

"Yes."

"Okay, so, if you could control the strategy 100% of the time, you would truly only need one strategy for each op (mission) is that right?"

He didn't answer me—our eyes locked. There was a moment where we both didn't say a word, and there's a flash gut reaction that happened where I thought, "This is the one guy in the room I do *not* want to piss off...". The point though was too strong to back away from.

I was right.

The big picture here is this: Strategy is linked directly to the outcome and results of what it is that we're trying to accomplish. If we could control the outcome of our strategy 100% of the time, you would genuinely only need one plan ever. You would never need a plan B.

The Navy SEAL operator was trained in the perspective that he described, and it's *brilliant*. Later in that session, he even mentioned to me: we were talking the same kind of strategy. We were thinking the same thought. We were just working from a different definition.

My definition of control is absolute. I'm only interested in what an athlete can control 100% of the time. Because I want an athlete to know what they can reliably put their trust, faith, hope, determination and energy fully invested into, to protect themselves from being left reeling and spinning if and when one of those uncontrollables break down.

Instead, what I want them to do, is to be resilient and tough-minded. In the face of adversity when those things pop up, I want

them to be prepared to the extent that, as my Navy operator said of
SEALs, "When plan A, B, and C goes wrong, it doesn't matter." The
reason SEALs can say that is they're trained to adapt, improvise, and
overcome.

Did you catch that?

Adapt. Improvise. Overcome.

They look for opportunities to take advantage of to get themselves
out of whatever situation they're in.

The takeaway is this: Don't get stuck with the uncontrollable.
Adapt. Overcome. Improvise. That's the mindset, as an athlete, you
should have and develop.

What does this look like for an athlete?

If you're a basketball player, Plan A might be getting all your shots
in because that is usually a strength for you. But when that's not
working out, and you're struggling with your shooting for whatever
reason at that moment, flex to plan B. Plan B could be to pass to
another teammate who you know is the next best shooter. Plan B
isn't working? Okay, now flex to plan C. You don't have a plan C? You
adapt on the fly. Maybe, in this case, you need to pick up your energy
on the defensive end and work on stopping the ball on a fast break,
boxing out your defender, or focusing your energy on sprinting back
on defense to get you more into the game.

You have to have a mindset of being willing and able to adapt your
strategy and of not getting hung up on one small, particular detail
that you can't seem to let go of.

Relinquish control of the things that you were actually never in
control of. Focus on something you can control: your ability to adapt.

We've all heard Murphy's Law: if something *can* go wrong, it *will*
go wrong. So have the mental agility to make that switch, to let go
of the things that anger and frustrate you. If you can't control them,
why are you wasting all your mental energy, stamina and focus on
those things?

To use another SEAL example, consider the capture of Osama
Bin Laden. The movie, "Zero Dark Thirty" released a few years ago
showed what took place.

SEAL Team Six flew in two Black Hawk helicopters, in Pakistan, to capture/kill Bin Laden in a compound. They had strong intelligence that he was there, along with several high-value targets. The plan to infiltrate the compound called for one Black Hawk to land on the outside, in an empty field.

The other Black Hawk helicopter was going to land inside the gates of the compound, but it clipped the edge of the wall. That aircraft went spiraling 13 feet down and crashed in the courtyard. Nobody was hurt, and the mission went on. But, now there's a downed Black Hawk in the middle of a residential neighborhood in the middle of the night.

SEALs being SEALs, they had a contingency plan for that. They flew in another helicopter. They were prepared, ready to overcome and adapt.

Here's something to ask yourself: As an athlete, when was the last time you did that? When was a time you were counting on your strategy, it let you down, and you bounced back with a new idea immediately?

TECHNIQUE

When I talk about technique, I like to talk about swimmers, because for them, technique is everything. A swimmer works on perfecting their stroke for the vast majority of their career—from childhood to the Olympics.

Unfortunately, I have to break it to them that their technique is **not** in their control 100%.

The first time I remember giving this session to an Olympic swimmer, her jaw was literally hanging open for about 60 seconds. That's what a shock it was to her, and what a loss, to understand that her technique was not under her control. I was met with eyes of part anger, confusion, shock, and anxiety. Yes, there were a lot of emotions and words exchanged and expressed.

To bring the point home to her, I said, "Remember, for the sake of this activity I only care about what you can control 100% of the time. Have you ever messed up your stroke just one time? Just once?"

"Yeah."

"Well, if you've messed up once but you can control it 100% of the time, why would you ever mess up?"

"Yeah," she said, "that makes sense."

"Well, the point is, can you do things to improve your technique?"

"Absolutely."

"Can you do things to be more consistent?"

"Absolutely."

"We should strive for those things, instead of allowing poor technique control us."

It's not that I want athletes to ignore technique. Technique is important, even foundational.

But the part that I really want to hammer home with any athlete is this: when your technique fails, that's okay. Let it go; adapt; improvise; improve. Work hard at being better at it but have a mindset that says, "It's okay not to have perfect technique and to keep going anyway." You must not allow poor technique to influence your performance immediately. Not if you're focused on your effort, concentration, and attitude.

As another example, think about a flute player. Flutists' technique is all about working their mouth muscles.

As a flute player, you're always trying to work on your mouth muscles. The way you position your mouth and lips on the instrument is called your *embouchure*, which is a French term. Flutists work for years to be able to blow air precisely across the mouthpiece edge so that it goes into the column of the flute and vibrates and creates noise. It's essential, and it's easy to feel like it's under your control. You develop and train this ability, like any muscle.

But then one day, maybe you've gone to the dentist, and suddenly, oops, it's not quite in your control. Or someone clips you on a bus across the mouth by mistake, leaving bruising. Or, you get a cold sore. Sometimes your brain-muscle connection just doesn't fire to its full capacity. For any reason, suddenly your technique, your body, isn't 100% under your control anymore.

TEAMMATES, COACHES, OPPONENTS

Right about now, you might be feeling like we've gone through the wringer together.

We just exposed, all the ways we don't control things that we probably thought we did before this book, and we wrestled with each one. You may be feeling a bit lost, upset with me, confused, or maybe relieved? Emotions are a very necessary part of the process of learning and applying ACE.

Focusing now on teammates, coaches, and opponents, this one should be an easy one, right?

It should be, but it's one that we as human beings seem to struggle with a lot. How much energy and attention do we put into trying to control those around us—and how emotional do we get when it doesn't work?

I'm talking about getting frustrated because our teammates don't do the right thing, or we're trying to influence the coach in some way, or even trying to control the opponents, and we're getting mad because they ran a particular play and exposed our weakness.

In the big picture, all three of these things are outside of our control, yet how much energy and attention do we put towards them?

I have some idea of how much we get preoccupied with trying to control others because I'm the one that gets long emails in my inbox from upset players, parents or coaches when they're trying to control things that are flat out of their control.

This is not to knock emotions. We are emotional creatures, and that's an important aspect of any game, any specialty—the fervor and drive that you bring to it. The fact that you care about the outcome. The fact that you want to put in the time. Emotional investment is an important motivation and driving force.

But like any superpower, you have to learn to control it. An emotional response at the wrong time (like immediately after a game) or in response to the wrong trigger (losing control, for example) can send you and your team reeling. The key is to invest your emotion in the things you *can* control, not on exterior things like what other people think or how they behave, or even the outcome of the game.

What kind of an athlete isn't emotionally invested in the outcome of the game? A resilient athlete, that's who.

I spend a lot of my effort on redirecting athletes, coaches, parents, and teams back to working on the things that are within that Circle of Control—the things that really matter.

Dear reader, I want to encourage you to be aware of when you are feeling the pull of these uncontrollables. Because it really does feel like a pull—something pulling your attention out of yourself, away from yourself.

When you feel that pull, get back to the circle and put your attention and energy there. Start there.

When we redirect our attention to the things we can control, the most meaningful things, we give ourselves the best chance to cut through the crap and put the most important things first. It's like you're getting into an emotional power stance—bracing yourself so that you can be unshakeable in the face of every distraction and preoccupation.

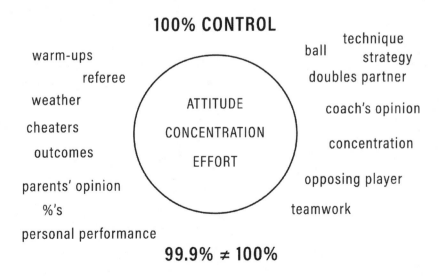

Having gone through these five factors, your circle of control shouldn't be very crowded anymore. Maybe you started out with quite a few things inside the circle, but throughout this chapter, you rethought a few of them and moved them outside. There should really just be three things in there at this point.

In the next chapter, I'll discuss those three things and why, if you shift your focus to them, you can change your life.

THE GROUND RULES:

1. Be prepared to re-evaluate old habits and assumptions.
2. Don't be afraid to disagree. Critical thinking is an important part of this process.
3. Be determined, patient and consistent; it may take time to see results once you start applying these concepts.
4. Maintain an open, teachable mind.

FIVE

ACE WITHIN THE CIRCLE OF CONTROL

THE GROUND RULES:

1. Be prepared to re-evaluate old habits and assumptions.
2. Don't be afraid to disagree. Critical thinking is an important part of this process.
3. Be determined, patient and consistent; it may take time to see results once you start applying these concepts.
4. Maintain an open, teachable mind.

What is, then, left in the middle of your Circle of Control? There are just three factors that should still be there: Attitude, Concentration, and Effort. Here is why each of those factors, and only those factors, is within your control.

100% CONTROL

ATTITUDE

CONCENTRATION

EFFORT

ATTITUDE

You may be thinking, *Trevor, I wouldn't say that I control my attitude 100% of the time, without fail. I have off days and bad days like anyone else.* Well, let's examine that idea a little closer.

Recall a time when you felt that your attitude was out of your control. For some, this will be a day when you were hungry or tired, or your training hit a plateau, and you just felt stuck in this cranky, frustrated kind of mood. Maybe it's an interaction with your siblings or parents that threw you off, or some annoying habit that bugs you and starts your day on the wrong foot. "My sister comes in my room in the morning, yanks the curtains open, and says it's time for school, and it really annoys me, and I start my day grumpy." Or maybe you have a demanding coach who yells at you when you feel you haven't done anything wrong.

All of these examples show that life happens all around us, 24/7. These incidents, the ones that feel like they derail our attitude, are variables, and they happen everywhere we go, all the time. We don't control the variables, no, but we also should not let the variables control us.

Let me ask you something. Who controls you?

When I ask this question to a room of athletes, it tends to get very quiet. Of course. Who in their right mind would have an answer to that question?

In the animated movie *Inside Out*, a really brilliant film, there are about five or six characters who each represent a different emotion of a girl. They're in charge of her, they decide how she will feel and what she will do.

At first glance, this sounds like a weird idea. *It's a movie, Trevor. Everyone knows we don't have little people in our heads controlling us.*

Yet in those examples we just considered, we gave all of the power to these other people. It's my coach's fault that I'm grumpy. It's because of my parents. My sister and I had a fight this morning.

So when one of those variables pops up, when someone around you does something that bothers you, who is in control of your response?

You are.

Even when it feels like your reaction is an impulse, like getting angry at the drop of a hat. Even then.

It's your choice. No matter how fast things are happening, you always have the opportunity to take a breath and consider your next move. When you don't take that breath, and you react without thinking, that's also a choice.

A given situation may not be in your control, but your attitude is always a choice. It's 100% under your control, whether you choose to exercise that control or not. When you have a bad day, and we all do, you can still decide to make some kind of improvement in your attitude throughout the day. You'll end up with more good days than not, as long as your goal is to be deliberate about your attitude each day.

The amount of improvement you can make in your life is directly influenced by what you spend your time and energy controlling. If your mental space is a battlefield, and these external forces that affect you are on the other side of the battlefield, then your goal is to extend the territory that you control as far as you can. You want to own as much of that battlefield as possible. Push the line back. Expand your boundary. Take back the control of things that you can control, things that you've ceded to others, like your attitude.

The question is: how good do you want to be? What would you be willing to do to see your next improvement as an athlete? Because this technique isn't asking all that much. At this point we're just talking about a mental shift. If it will help you get better, Isn't that worth it?

Studies show that your attitude is one of the greatest predictors of success in life.

Dr. Alan Zimmerman, a world-renowned leader and expert in attitude, who has authored dozens of great books and delivered too many keynotes to mention, shared a study in his book, *Pivot*, that is one of my all-time favorite citations.

The study is from Dr. Martin Seligman's work and book, Learned Optimism. The premise goes like this: Seligman does research on adults over 20 years. The participants are divided into two groups, the first of which is made up of people who chose their career because they believed they'd make a lot of money. That group, Group A, has 1245 people or 83% of the total participants. The other group, Group B, is made up of people who chose their career because they enjoyed what they did. That group was just 255 people or 17% of the total participants.

Fast forward 20 years later, out of those 1500 total participants, which group produced the most millionaires?

If you're like most of the athletes I train, they want to jump to the group who chose their careers because they believed they would make a lot of money. To say they're surprised when they realized more millionaires were produced from the other group would be an understatement. 101 total millionaires were created, but 100 of them came from the group who chose their careers because they enjoyed their profession. Not only that, but 70% of the millionaires did not have college degrees, and out of every person in the group who was a CEO, 70% of them graduated in the bottom half of their classes. You can imagine the looks on the faces of elite athletes when they hear that.

Based on the outcomes of the study, Seligman concludes that a positive attitude is a crucial trait of successful people. I'd say that's a reasonable conclusion.

The word "attitude" can be overused and abused to the point that it can lose meaning. If you've ever been that troublemaking kid in class who was always told you have a "bad attitude," I can imagine the suspicion you might have towards this term. In this chapter, I'll explain in more detail what I mean by "attitude."

But this study shows that it's not just fluff. It's not just something motivational speakers tell their audiences. It's a real factor, and it has a massive impact on your ability to live a successful life, whatever that means to you.

I want to take a minute to acknowledge that this study defined "success" as becoming a millionaire. Are there ways to measure success other than just dollar signs? Absolutely...but what was that guided those adults to their financial success or failures from the core? I would argue, their attitude. Consider your attitude like your compass.

"It is your attitude, more than your aptitude, that will determine your altitude."

In other words, what really matters is the way you look at, and interact with, the world, not how smart or gifted you are.

So, it's a good thing that this key significant factor, this major influence throughout our lives, is something that *is* under your control.

A coach I immensely respected growing up always said, "An athlete with a piss-poor attitude can expect to get piss-poor results."

Take a look at some of the athletes that you look up to, even at the high school or college level. Does their attitude reflect your personal beliefs? Because if not, you should find a role model whose attitude does.

But they're successful, you may be thinking. They must be doing something right!

The ACE teaching method is not about following success at all costs. I don't believe that's the way to train the best athletes. Results are fleeting and superficial, they don't tell you what's really going on inside that athlete over the long-term. You can be an absolutely toxic person and enjoy temporary success as an athlete, but sooner or later, those problems will catch up with you and with anyone who emulates your behavior.

Plus, if all you look at is your outcomes, you end up on the "results rollercoaster": the coaching term for someone whose mood is determined by their last game or training session. When you're doing well, you're on top of the world, and when you're not doing well, you're awful to be around. No one wants to work with that athlete. That emotional volatility tends to spill over into a career that is up and down, unpredictable and hit-or-miss, whereas athletes with solid attitudes and strong self-control tend to perform more consistently.

Besides, as far as I'm concerned, focusing on results is putting the cart before the horse. As I mentioned in the earlier chapters, you are more than your success, and your life is more significant than your athletic achievements. When your athletic career is over—and everyone's career comes to an end someday—you still need to have a life. You still need to have values, skills, and interests outside of playing the game. Once you've developed your habits, they develop you—so you need to make sure if you're following a ruthless, no-holds-barred, borderline toxic, results-driven success, that you're okay with those values leaking over into your personal life and your relationships. Because they will.

Ask yourself, are you willing to chase results even if it means sacrificing your personal ethics and character? Or do you want to follow a teaching method that will help instill true strength and integrity in every area of your life?

If you think of an athlete that truly inspires you, one that doesn't just impress you, but really inspires you with who they are as a person, I think you'll find it all boils down to one main attribute. It's called attitude.

Attitude means keeping your perspective, thinking constructively, acting instead of reacting, and weathering the storm instead of getting pulled along with it.

You still have emotions, but no matter how emotional you are, you have the ability to maintain enough self-control to show respect for yourself and those around you. When things go wrong, you're not the one throwing blame. You're the one self-correcting, getting your equilibrium back, taking the learnings from the loss and bringing them to your training session the next day.

In the sports industry, it can be common to think that it's natural for athletes to get angry and lose their temper, throw things, cuss people out. It's all part of the passion of an elite performer. Well, I can tell you in practical terms, that's not the case. That's another Hollywood lie. The psychological terminology I'll use is "catharsis," and the theory behind it is that you're working through your anger by taking it out on those objects or people. By punching the wall, or kicking a trash can, you're making yourself feel better.

The only problem with this theory is that this type of catharsis doesn't work. In fact, studies show that going on a rant, or hitting something, leaves you feeling angrier than before because you've worked yourself up. Remember what I just mentioned about habits up above? You develop your habits and then your habits will develop you. If you're in the habit of getting angry, anger will likely be a strong habit that will develop for a long time.

So as a coach, I don't buy the myth that it's acceptable for athletes to throw temper tantrums. These athletes, these top performers who get so angry they throw their golf clubs into the woods or break their tennis rackets, fundamentally lack self-control. The athletes who can control themselves and refrain from abusing inanimate objects are the ones who are likely to keep a cool head during the game as well.

Here's a personal anecdote to show the power of attitude.

Do you know the story of St. Paul in prison? The one where he and Silas were beaten and thrown into jail. Paul had exorcized a demon from a slave girl who had been telling fortunes. Without the demon, she couldn't tell fortunes anymore, and she was useless to her masters. So they gathered a crowd and attacked the two apostles, beat them with rods, and threw them in jail.

The Bible says that Paul and Silas spent the night praying and singing hymns, with the other prisoners listening in. Can you imagine singing songs after you've been savagely beaten?

Suddenly, there was an earthquake, the doors of the jail were thrown open, and everyone's chains came loose. When the jailer saw the prison doors open, he thought all of the prisoners had run away.

He knew he would be facing a huge fine or punishment so the jailer was ready to kill himself until he heard Paul's voice:

"Don't harm yourself! We are all here!"

They had not even bothered to run away. That's how little the external circumstance of the jail mattered to Paul and Silas. They were in prison, beaten and in chains, but they were still calm and in control. In their minds, they were there because God wanted them to be, not because anyone forced them.

In Romans 12:2, Paul says:

"Do not be conformed to this world, but be transformed with the renewing of your mind so that you may prove what the will of God is and that is good, acceptable, and perfect."

What that verse says to me is that if you allow yourself to focus on the world and what the world tells you is important, expect to gain bitterness and distress and frustration, because you can't control the things of the world. Instead, Paul tells you to have your mind renewed and transformed by essentially putting on a Godly perspective of looking at things from an eternal view, not mortal. He's saying, "Don't be conformed to the world. Be transformed with your mind."

To put it another way: 1 John 2:15 says,

"Do not love the world or the things in this world. If anyone loves the world, the love of the Father is not in him."

This comes back to that old-fashioned word that I used in an earlier chapter: idolatry.

Idolatry means pinning all of your hopes on false idols, objects that can't possibly fulfill your needs. It has a particular significance for Christians, but even outside of that, anyone can see that if you pin your hopes on something unreliable, something that's going to let you down, sooner or later you'll be disappointed.

So if your whole world falls apart because you lose a game, not just for a few hours or one night while you decompress, but for weeks and months, you need an attitude check. Your compass needs recalibrating. Because one game shouldn't have the power to destroy you, not if you're focusing on the things you can control.

CONCENTRATION

Who is in control of you?

The obvious answer is: you. You're in control of yourself.

So if you're in control of yourself, then you're in control of your attitude. Which means you're in control of what you choose to focus on.

When I say this to athletes, the number one response I get is, "But Trevor, I can't control what people say about me. I get distracted."

First of all, good job. You've identified that you can't control other people. But you're still saying that you can't control distractions.

Who's responsible for bringing your concentration back to the task in the moment after you got distracted? You are.

Distractions are inevitable. The point is that we can condition ourselves to come right back to the task at hand, every time. Come back to what we need to focus on and eliminate those distracting thoughts.

To bring this home, I like to run the following experiment.

If you were one of my students, I would start by telling you I was a college baseball player and that I am very accurate throwing objects, so you should trust me. I would take a pen or marker and tell you, "Whatever you do, you're not going to flinch."

As you're standing there, staring at me in confusion, I hurl the marker with great velocity right past your head, inches from your right ear. Would you flinch or blink? About 95% of the time, the athlete doesn't flinch! Would you believe it? The ones that do typically freak out and yell in shock that I threw a pen or marker at them. I have to remind them that if I had intended on hitting them, I would have.

The pen is like a distraction. It comes right at you, right at your head in this case, and you have a choice how to respond. If you've conditioned yourself not to react, you won't.

When we are distracted, it's our choice to come back to refocus on the here and now. No one else controls your level of concentration. It's 100% your choice…100% of the time.

Remember the circle of control.

The original question was, *can you* control these things 100%, not *do you*. We want to dial into this "can you" part of the query, because that's where growth awaits.

Will you be distracted from time to time? Of course! We're human! Will you daze off in school? Church? Your friends having a pointless conversation that you couldn't care less about? A coach or a parent rambling on and on about the loss or the great win? Of course. Losing concentration is to be expected. But whose decision is it to dial back into the present moment again?

If you need help with that one, it's you. It's your choice.

Concentration is an endurance skill. You develop it over time, with practice. It's something you can get better at, and by getting better at concentrating, you're getting better at controlling your ability to focus and be locked in. You're placing it where you want instead of having it pulled in different directions by external forces.

Have you ever been at a party or in a group of people, where you didn't want to be anymore? Somewhere where you stayed because you thought, *I can't go.* You thought you couldn't go because your friends were there, or you were afraid people would make fun of you if you left—but if you had a choice you would have liked to go?

With the power of attitude and concentration comes the ability to say, "This isn't where I want to be. This isn't my thing," and to simply leave. You had the choice to leave all along, and now you're just taking it. You're following through with what you want to do, your intrinsic motivation, instead of letting other people make your choices for you.

EFFORT

Athletes ask me all the time: "How can I give effort? What does that mean?"

I often hear coaches ask their athletes for "110%". What does that even mean? If I'm asked for 100%, and I give it my best, and then a coach says this time I need to give 110%, how is that even possible? How can I give better than my best?

The coach who asks for 100% knows that you have more to give, that you have more gas in the tank, that you can keep going. When we're at our "perceived limit," we're typically only at about 30-40% of our maximum threshold.

Navy SEALs train for up to two years to become SEALs. In BUD/S (Basic Underwater Demolition/SEAL School), there are stories of guys being so sleep deprived that they've fallen asleep while rowing, or while running, keeping pace with everyone else, but fast asleep. The body is capable of amazing things under pressure.

So why aren't we all Navy SEALs? I believe it's the mind that limits us, not just the body. As we approach our threshold of effort, we start to feel pain, fear, and anxiety. We don't want to hurt ourselves. We question if it's worth it. Elite performers are those who can accept those messages from the brain and choose to keep going anyway.

Effort is determined by how hard you work, and how hard you try. Similar to attitude and concentration, you are in control of how much effort you put in. If you don't get many opportunities in games, that's okay. When you are given your opportunities, give your best effort, 100% of the time. Effort lies within you.

How much effort you put in is a choice decided by you, and only you. How good do you want to be? What are you willing to do to give yourself the best chance to be as successful you can be? Even on a day when you're sick or injured, you may not be able to perform at 100%, but you can sure give 100% of your effort.

Does your coach start you? Bench you? Not even look your way anymore? Doesn't matter...does it? You can't control the coach. Mom and Dad can't control the coach. No one else can coach you better than you because only you can choose to keep going. Only you can decide to push through. A coach can ask for that effort from you, but only you can feel what you're capable of.

I am a mental coach, but you can be a better mental coach for yourself than I ever could. I can provide you with the mental skills, the habits, and levels of effort to give when the situation demands it, but you are the one who shapes your attitude, your concentration, and your effort—and that makes you a better and more effective coach for yourself than I could ever be.

Here's one for you to think about—especially if you're a coach. Head Coach Geno Auriemma from UConn Women's Basketball is famous, an absolute legend when it comes to his coaching philosophies, championship banners he's won, athletes that went on to play professionally, blue-chip players that commit as early as freshmen in high school to his program. UConn Women's Basketball is feared, partly I believe, because of his ACE.

ESPN did a *Behind the Scenes* piece on him, to film his practices and see how UConn basketball and Coach Geno works. In this documentary, addressing his team, Coach Geno gives the following message calm, steady, and seriously:

> *"The difference between a good player and a great player is great players don't get tired. They just don't.*
>
> *And what makes them great is when the good players get tired, the great player kicks their ass. That's the difference.*
>
> *So everyday you're working on that. Everyday you're working on that.*
> *We can coach ball screens and passing into the post and cutting and playing defense…we're not here to coach your energy level and your effort. That's a given.*
>
> *You wouldn't be here if I had to coach that. That's what other coaches have to do is coach energy. We don't. You all know that."*

What does Coach Geno know that we don't? I would argue he doesn't know anything different, but his expectations and what he demands from his athletes is different. He knows what a powerful predictor effort can be for a team's success.

When UConn is up 50 points against a team that doesn't have a hope against them, you watch. You'll see them diving on loose balls, sprinting to complete layups, running back on defense, giving their all for a game that's in the bag. Their coach demands that from them, and they give 100% effort right till the end, no matter what.

Whatever you're doing, you can always do more. You can always do better. If you're looking to improve and you're getting frustrated because you're not getting better, take a look at everything you're doing. Somewhere, you'll find something you can do better. Whether it's your studies, your sleep habits, what you eat, or a completely different area of effort—like working on getting along with your teammates—there's always a way to improve. That belief system becomes a way of life, where you learn to always be on the lookout for the next improvement, always accepting the next challenge. Even if it's just to get 1% better that day.

This isn't just about sports anymore. You can get better in every area of your life. Each of us has things that we know we're not great at, where we know we're not doing our best. We just get lazy, or we get into denial, and we don't make the effort.

But what if you just chose to make the effort? Face that weak area head-on and do something better? Keep a cleaner house; build a better relationship with your family or friends; study harder. Any job you do, any task before you, do it well. Not because others are asking or demanding, but because it's who you are. It's in your nature to try your hardest because that's what you practice every day.

This doesn't mean you should become some sort of machine, pushing yourself 24 hours a day. Rest takes effort, too. Resting properly, that is—turning off Netflix, turning off your phone, and concentrating on rest. Asking yourself, *How could this rest be more effective? What could I do better?*

The principles in this book are a way to understand, direct, and hold yourself accountable to the amount of effort that you put into your life. Once you see life in this way—as a set of things that you can control—and once you commit to putting all of your effort—the real 100%—into those things, you will be able to achieve astonishing, transformational change in your life.

Make a decision. It needs to be a yes or no. From now on, you either do something 100%, or you don't do it. As Yoda says, "Do or do not; there is no try." Because using the word "try" gives you an out, a chance to back down. Notice, I'm not saying you have to be successful 100% of the time. Effort doesn't guarantee success. Even the best athletes lose a game now and then. But putting in 100% effort means you committed. You showed up and you did everything in your power, focusing on the things you know you can control, to achieve your aim. That's the ACE Method.

THE GROUND RULES:

1. Be prepared to re-evaluate old habits and assumptions.
2. Don't be afraid to disagree. Critical thinking is an important part of this process.
3. Be determined, patient and consistent; it may take time to see results once you start applying these concepts.
4. Maintain an open, teachable mind.

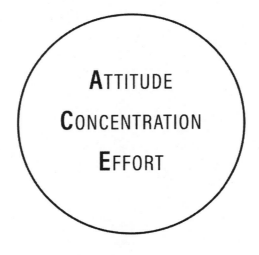

SIX

REVISITING THE CIRCLE OF CONTROL

THE GROUND RULES:

1. Be prepared to re-evaluate old habits and assumptions.
2. Don't be afraid to disagree. Critical thinking is an important part of this process.
3. Be determined, patient and consistent; it may take time to see results once you start applying these concepts.
4. Maintain an open, teachable mind.

Prepare yourself for the discomfort of discovering that you were wrong about something. This chapter will walk you through the transformational aspect of the Circle of Control exercise. But transformation can be uncomfortable, so bear with me as I share with you what I hope you'll find to be an exciting new perspective on your game and yourself as an athlete.

As always, disagreement is welcomed, and I will help you in this chapter to follow that sense of dissent and resistance, to find a place where things are changing inside yourself.

Emptying your cup is also vital for this chapter. If you find yourself encountering a lot of resistance to the ideas I present here, think of this as an experiment. Apply my ideas, just for the time it takes to read this chapter, and follow my logic, even if only for the sake of argument. See where you end up. I think you'll be pleasantly surprised.

At SPIRE Institute, a US Olympic & Paralympic Site in Geneva, Ohio, where I gave the lesson on controllables to the Navy SPECWAR Scouts I mentioned earlier, I also had the pleasure to work with some very talented FINA sponsored athletes in 2014-16 training for the 2016 Olympics in Rio.

Now, as I've mentioned, swimmers particularly hate the Circle of Control exercise. I remember doing it with four swimmers in particular, from Fiji, Uruguay, Cook Islands (New Zealand), and Guam. Each individual had put 12+ items in their respective circles. My eyes were as big as the Olympic-sized pool when I saw their papers. But I just took a deep breath and said, "Well guys... wow. We've got a lot of work to do. Let's get after it."

In the end, two out of those four athletes went on to represent their respective countries in the 2016 Olympics, and all four represented their countries in different national competitions during the 2016 lead up to the Rio Olympic Games. It was incredible to watch the transformation as they released their prior assumptions about what they could control, and instead learned, understood, and applied the ACE method. Until then, they were living entirely for technique, results, and other people's opinions. Amazingly these athletes got it, to the point that they started thinking differently about their sport and their lives.

Why does this simple exercise bring out such strong emotions in the people who work through it? I have a couple theories.

When people are working through the first steps of the exercise, listing all of the things they think they control and placing them in the middle of the circle, they are building a symbol of their own identity as an athlete. That circle on the page, with the items listed, comes to represent who they are and what they can do. Then when I direct people to move things out, they feel that sense of self weakens.

These things the athletes thought they could control, that they thought were part of who they were, are being stripped away.

It reminds me of the story of Lee Strobel, the man who wrote *The Case for Christ,* a famous Christian apologetics book (apologetics refers to a defense or justification, so this is a book that justifies and defends Christianity). Strobel was a journalist and spiritual skeptic who decided to investigate the Christian faith after his wife converted. He interviewed thirteen evangelical scholars, asking tough questions and demanding evidence about Christian beliefs, like the birth and resurrection of Jesus Christ, the authenticity of the Bible and the veracity of the New Testament. In the end, Strobel concluded that the evidence in favor of Christ and Christianity was overwhelming. He converted to Christianity and is now a pastor.

When I think of Strobel cross-examining all of those Christian scholars, himself a skeptic, and feeling convicted by each of their robust and logical answers, I think my approach with the Circle of Control has a little bit in common with Strobel. I ask my athletes tough questions, too—questions that are meant to challenge the very foundations of who they are and how they play their game. But with each question I ask, I peel away another one of their false assumptions, and I can see that bit by bit these athletes are being convinced, too. They're slowly realizing, one by one, that they don't control the things they thought they did. These athletes are discovering a profound truth about themselves, a truth with a capital T, a truth that has profound spiritual roots.

Remember: ***Do not conform to the pattern of this world, but be transformed by the renewing of your mind.***

Apply it to your life as best as you can because that message is so universal and so profound. This world will try to fit you in a box, will try to dictate what you can do, how you should think and act, what you can believe. As inspirational as celebrities and athletes can be, idolizing them allows that admiration to set the narrative for what you can achieve. If you worship LeBron, you'll want to live out his life. Not yours. Even if your life could be better, or different, you won't be looking for the real opportunities that might exist for you.

You'll instead be focused on looking for the opportunities that got LeBron where he is.

Don't conform. Be transformed.

Ultimately, each thing that is outside of your control that you think you can control is actually something that controls you. Let that sink in for a moment.

It's something that preoccupies you, draws your focus, directs how you spend your time and how you make your decisions as an athlete. For each item that gets moved out of the circle, you are actually gaining your freedom back. It feels like you're losing something, but all you're letting go of is the bars of the jail that you were holding onto. Now there's much less to hold on to, so you're free.

Right now, I'd like for you to pause, check in with yourself and take a look at your circle of control. If you are shocked to count up all of the items that have moved out of the circle of control, you might be feeling some resistance to this teaching method, perhaps even some powerful emotions. That's ok. Let's take stock of those.

GROWTH OPPORTUNITIES

The Circle of Control exercise brings up a lot of strong responses. But even if they feel negative, those thoughts and emotions represent a powerful step forward, that you are really engaged with the exercise and learning something from it. New growth can be uncomfortable, even painful, but it's always productive. I'll walk you through acknowledging and processing your reactions to this challenging exercise.

First, check in on your mental state and your attitude right now. Where are you at? What are you concentrating on right now? Are you bitter? Do you still want to fight me on the Circle? Are you an empty cup or are you spilling over?

Whatever kind of resistance you may be feeling, I'd like you to trust it, trust the process and go with it for now. Old, established ideas are being displaced.

Transformation is uncomfortable.

If you feel you've just been challenged with some of the beliefs you've had for and held a long time…then step up to the plate.

You're an athlete, and this is a challenge. What do we do when we're challenged? We step up, we get ready, we fully engage. Because there's a lot more coming.

Let's debrief for a quick moment. Think about how complex you have made your sport over the years, attempting to control things that you actually couldn't. Right now, I'd like to give you an opportunity to put on a growth mindset.

Pick one of the most positive and influential aspects or moments of your sporting, coaching, or parenting career. Got it?

Seriously, stop and visualize it.

Now in that moment...dial into your A (attitude). I would imagine it was positive and optimistic.

Next is C (concentration): were you concentrating on the bad officiating, the other team's strategy, or even having absolutely perfect technique? Doubtful—I would believe that you were focused and concentrated on play-to-play and flexing when bad things were happening. You were overcoming distractions and adversities that had popped up. In that moment, I would almost guarantee that you were choosing to concentrate on the right things rather than be distracted.

Finally, check in with your E (effort). Where were your efforts at? I can imagine that your effort was similar to A & C.

Now pick one of the more recent moments in sport that didn't go your way.

Were you attempting to control the results too much? Were you too focused on technique and percentages? Are you guilty of placing blame on your teammates for missing the shots? The pass? The bad reaction? Could you have used ACE to redirect you? I challenge you to keep reading, learning, understanding, but most importantly— get ready to apply it!

THE (MODIFIED) GROUND RULES:

1. ACE takes patience, consistency, and determination.
2. Be honest and open.
3. Empty your cup. You must be coachable and humble.

SEVEN

FOUNDATIONS OF A MENTALLY TOUGH ATHLETE

THE GROUND RULES

1. Be prepared to re-evaluate old habits and assumptions.
2. Don't be afraid to disagree. Critical thinking is an important part of this process.
3. Be determined, patient and consistent; it may take time to see results once you start applying these concepts.
4. Maintain an open, teachable mind.
5. Empty your cup

In this chapter, we're going to talk about breaking bad habits, learning new behaviors, refocusing our attention, and learning how to be deliberate and purposeful in every aspect of your game. Unlearning old behaviors, and learning new ones, takes a considerable amount of time and investment. Any practice or skill that's covered in this chapter will probably take some extra time to sink in and start to make a difference. Keep in mind, this chapter deals with changes and practices that really do affect your whole life.

Be honest and open.

Empty your cup. You must be coachable and humble.

The ACE method is about having a solid foundation for your game. So first, let's talk about the importance of that solid foundation.

There is an excellent story from the Bible about this called the story of the Two Builders. Jesus told the story to his followers to explain that his teachings could be the foundation for their whole lives.

> *Anyone who hears and obeys these teachings of mine is like a wise person who built a house on solid rock. Rain poured down, rivers flooded, and winds beat against that house. But it did not fall, because it was built on solid rock.*

> *Anyone who hears my teachings and doesn't obey them is like a foolish person who built a house on sand. The rain poured down, the rivers flooded, and the winds blew and beat against that house. Finally, it fell with a crash.*

Let's think of your athletic career as a house that you're going to build. First, you need to decide where it's going to go, and then you can start putting in your foundation. Would you rather build on sand, or on rock?

I used to take groups of students out to Lake Erie when I lived in the Great Lakes region. Using some sand castle tools, I would build a small sand castle right near the water's edge.

I would ask the athletes, "How long is it going to take for my castle to fall?" They would start making bets because, as we all know, a house built on sand will fall, it's just a matter of time. It's the same thing with your athletic career if it's not built on the principles of ACE.

After taking bets on the sand castle, I would collect a few heavy stones and cluster them together on the beach, and build the sand castle again on top of the rocks. I would ask again: "Now how long is it going to take my castle to fall? Will it fall easily?" My students would say, "No."

So I would ask, "Why not?"

And they'd said, "Because that's a solid foundation."

That's what ACE is.

ACE is a solid foundation that you can build on top of. Without that solid foundation, pretty soon you'll start to notice cracks in the walls, the roof might cave in, the ceiling might begin to collapse. So I ask my students, "What kind of a house is that to live in?" Some of the younger athletes will say, "Well, that's a messy one." I'll say, "That's right. And how messy are your athletic lives, in a way, when you're attempting to control things that you can't control?"

To explain it another way, here's a visual representation.

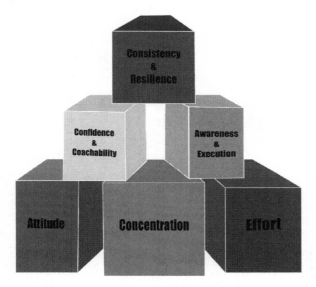

This is my personal theory on different aspects of what makes a mentally tough athlete. The components of ACE are all at the bottom. That's because they're foundational—they hold everything else up.

To be very clear, this is *not* an exhaustive list of everything that goes into making a mentally tough athlete. Not even close. What you can see, though, is a glimpse of how the ACE components are at the root of everything, and many other things depend on them.

As you move towards the top of the pyramid, you start seeing qualities and traits that are built on top of the solid ACE foundation— that is what will begin to fall apart if the foundation disappears.

An athlete isn't going to be very confident or coachable if they don't have their attitude straightened out. And if they're not coachable, they're not going to be very consistent in their performance, because they're not taking instruction from the experts around them.

In this chapter, I'll work through each of the ACE components and explain why they are foundational to a mentally tough athlete. I'll show you that the key for mastering each of these components is learning to be *purposeful* about it.

You choose your attitude, your concentration and your effort—it doesn't just happen. The ACE components are things you can learn to direct and control on purpose. I'll also teach some mental skills that athletes can improve on in each of the ACE areas.

ATTITUDE

Attitude sits at the bottom of the pyramid, under Confidence & Coachability. If you pull that out, how long are you going to stay confident and coachable? Your house may stay up for a little bit, but guess what? There's a wall of your home missing, and you're going to feel it. You can fake confidence for a little while, but with your first or second loss, or the first or second times you struggle to learn a technique, your insecurities will soon come out. Real confidence comes from an attitude that's humble, teachable, curious, and optimistic.

The right attitude isn't something you just wake up with or are born with. It's not even necessarily something you learn as you grow up; Lord knows I've met plenty of adults who still haven't figured out their attitude. Attitude is something we learn to choose and control over time, by investing our effort to get better at it.

As I mentioned in the previous chapter, **attitude** is one of the most influential factors and predictors of success.

One term that you've probably already seen in this book, and that will appear more often is *thinking trap*. Thinking Traps refers to a pattern of thought or thinking that leads to a state of anxiety, frustration, confusion, doubt, or setback where the thought and pattern can immobilize and paralyze us.

It's a thought that could be irresistible—like when you're angry, and you think about getting justice or getting revenge—but the eventual outcome won't satisfy you or benefit you in the long term. That's why it's a trap—it's something that lures your mind to a particular idea or plan, but ultimately it will hurt you or at least waste your energy. If you're a golfer and you have a 2-stroke lead going into the final hole and you tell yourself before you tee off, "I can't give up this lead on this last hole." You've walked right into a very common thinking trap here—outcome-based thinking.

That's a very common thinking trap related to attitude. If our attitude isn't solid, anytime you run into challenges or adversity, you'll have an impulsive, knee-jerk, emotional reaction—even an explosive, angry reaction, at times. That happens when you allow your actions and mood to be dictated by whatever events happen to come your way. Like all thinking traps, this reaction feels good, it feels productive. At least you're doing *something*, even if what you're doing is throwing a tantrum in your coach's office. But like all thinking traps, it gets you nowhere. Reacting without thinking just makes things worse.

The ACE method teaches you how to choose your attitude regardless of the things that come up in your life. If you decide on what your attitude will be, you're generally putting yourself in a much better position to respond well.

The allure of the thinking trap is that it seems to offer you some emotional satisfaction. Those athletes were fixated on getting revenge and being angry because it felt good. But it won't satisfy them in the long-term.

Emotional reactions run down and need to be recharged. You're angry now, and that anger seems to be driving you; this angry reaction feels productive, as if you're doing something useful. But you'll tire of it, and then you'll need something else to whip up your anger again. An athlete can't be caught up in this cycle. If you're going to perform at your best, consistently, then you need a constant, reliable source of energy.

Do me a favor. Think of a situation in life, when you made a recent and strong emotional decision or responded emotionally to a situation. How did that turn out? Chances are, it didn't turn out well (meaning you could have handled the situation better), and typically we regret those decisions as those conversations usually don't go exactly how we would like.

What does that tell us? It tells us that we are much better human beings and people when we are thinking our way through life critically and rationally, methodically working our way towards an objective, not just emotionally reacting and shooting from the hip.

This is not to say that you can't be angry. People get mad sometimes; we're all human beings. Even in the face of loss or grief, there still is a level of emotion that needs to be expressed. Having emotion is okay. Going through the stages of grief is okay.

But you must not let that anger or that grief take the wheel and start driving. Before you react out loud, just pause, slow down, and choose your attitude. The outcomes will likely be a lot better down the road if you're being deliberate and measured, as opposed to just being unhinged driven by emotion.

The anger, or whatever emotion you're feeling, is information. You need to take it and reflect on it and choose in a calm moment what you're going to do next. Think about what's making you angry and what you can do about that, and place your focus back where it belongs, which is on the internal things that you can control.

MENTAL SKILL #1: SLOW DOWN

A professor of mine used to have a saying: "Hit the pause button." You would be talking to her, and suddenly she'd say, "No, hit the pause button right now. Rewind, replay that. Let's think." She was referring to the DVR—how you can pause and rewind live TV. If you miss something, you hit pause, rewind and look at it again, maybe in slow motion so you can really see what's happening.

My professor was getting us to analyze our ideas and reactions, to take a second look at something we had just said, and to examine why we said that and where that idea came from.

When you hit the pause button, rewind, and play it in slow motion, you get a chance to objectively see what's happening, amidst your emotions, and understand why you're feeling those things. Where did that reaction come from? Did you make an assumption about someone else instead of looking at the facts? It gives you a chance to actually direct yourself rather than letting external forces direct you, like a ball in a pinball machine, knocked from one emotion to the next.

This applies to huge emotions and small ones too—small decisions, little things that happen. This mental skill is about breathing, slowing down, thinking. Take a moment to hit pause and rewind on our impulses and reactions.

MENTAL SKILL #2: CONTINGENCY PLANNING

A fire drill is an example of a contingency plan: you know ahead of time what to do if a fire ever happens at your school. If there's a fire, then you are prepared to find the nearest exit.

Just like practicing a fire drill, you can prepare what you'll do ahead of time when you're hit by an emotional situation so that in the moment when your critical thinking skills might not be the best, you don't have to come up with a response on the spot. You  have one ready to go, and you know you can trust it because you planned it out when you were calm and thinking straight.

Prepare for possible situations by creating IF/THEN statements:

If ____x____ happens, then you will do _____y_____.

IF/THEN statements are a tremendous opportunity for you to be prepared to conquer situations and challenges before they arise. When the adversity does strike, you'll have a much better chance to flex your optimistic muscles and focus on overcoming the trouble, not being stuck there.

Ultimately, as you'll see in my suggested responses at the end of this chapter, it really comes down to grounding yourself in the knowledge that whatever happens, you still have a job to do. You still have a purpose for being in that game or that practice, so you have to pull back into yourself, align your mind and body in the attitude and concentration that you choose, and direct your effort towards one specific goal.

CONCENTRATION

I define concentration as attention. In the ACE method, concentration is a question of where your attention is: inside or outside? On things you can control or stuff you can't? It's also about duration. How long can you concentrate for, without getting distracted?

Below is a diagram that I use to explain where we want our attention to be. It shows the three different states that our mind can be focusing on: past, present, and future. Our body is always in the present, of course, but your mind can wander to any of these three modes. Our worry and anxiety can be directed to any of these three things: something from the past, something happening now, or something that might happen in the future

As athletes, we are typically at our best when our mind and body are aligned together and tied to the present moment.

Imagine if you're that stick figure, and your body is in the middle column, but your head is over in the left or right column. That would be pretty painful, wouldn't you say? That's how simple this concept is. Your body and mind need to be aligned, which means your mind needs to join your body in the present moment, where you belong.

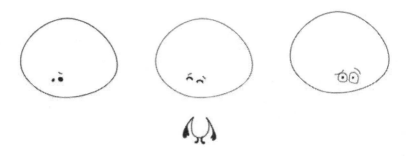

When you look back as an athlete and ask yourself, "What should I have done?" or "What next?", that can be a good thing for your game. But if you start fixating for an extended time on the past or the future, it can have an adverse effect. Dwelling on the past can lead to depression, and anticipating on the future can lead to anxiety and a worried state because you can't control those things, and you're not meant to.

...Do not worry about tomorrow; for tomorrow will care for itself. Each day has enough trouble of its own.—Matthew 6:34 (NASB)

My version of that verse, for athletes, would go like this:

Don't focus too far into the past; each day has enough trouble of its own. Stay focused on the task at hand. Stay focused on the present. Stay focused on what you've got to do.

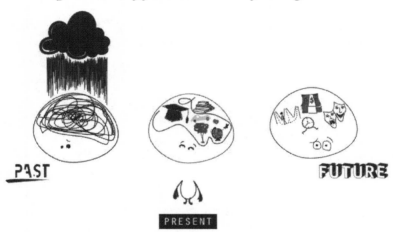

We all have moments where we think ahead or think back, and that's fine. It's okay to review the gameplay, it's okay to look forward and set goals for the future, it's okay to prep for things and to mentally create a strategy. But the importance of the concentration aspect of ACE is being able to concentrate on what you've got to do right in front of you. You can't let yourself *fixate* on anything in the past or the future, though, because if you do, all of those thoughts and feelings that you dwell on will become actions, and the actions will grow into behaviors, and the behaviors will become habits.

I was reading a book a few years ago about a Navy SEAL instructor. He was running some training in the pool, and he noticed one of the guys start to lock up and panic. He had become fixated on his past failures in the pool and was worried about how he would do in the future.

So the instructor said to him, "Three feet."

The guy looked up and said, "Excuse me?"

The instructor said, "Three feet. Control what you can control within a three feet radius around you. Everything else—let it go."

I like this version of the "three-foot world":

Be where your feet are.

When your mind and body are both focused on the present moment, you give yourself quicker opportunities to get in the zone, or in a flow state. When you're there, execution of skills or tasks seem effortless, and everything is easy. Things around you could be moving at a breakneck speed, but to you, it may feel slow, steady and calm. If I were to ask you at that moment, "What are you thinking about? What are you focused on?" You would most likely tell me things that are specifically tied to the present.

If an athlete has ADHD, my approach is to work with what you've got. You can allow yourself to be hindered by your disability, but we all have an ability to give our best effort at any given time, and that's only up to us. If you can only concentrate for three seconds at a time, that's okay. You can still work to improve from there. You may never be able to get to 10 reps of my Red Dot Concentration Activity (then again, almost no one can!) but you might be able to hold your concentration from three seconds to five seconds. If your condition can be treated with medication, that's great, that can help, but there is still an aspect of developing a skill that can and should happen. Remember, concentration is attention.

When I work with an athlete who has any kind of set limits on what they can and can't do, I want them to say, *I don't care where I'm at right now. It doesn't matter, because I'm going to get better from here. I'm going to improve, even if it's just 1%, even a fraction of a percent.*

We still need to quantify what that looks like and what that means to that individual, but I've never liked the feeling of just accepting what you have and being done with it. Life is way too short to just let it be that your starting point is going to be the same as your ending point, and to let that starting point define you.

Rather than focusing on the times that you struggle, notice those times where you're improving. Regardless of where you start, you can still find a flow state. What's a flow state? Here's an example.

I'm working with a major league baseball player right now. I was talking to him about being in the zone, and he said, "When I'm in the zone, I can feel the spin of the ball." I ask him to explain this to me a little more.

He said, "It's coming in at 95 miles an hour, but I can feel it coming. It looks like a pumpkin to me, it's so big. I can see and feel its spin."

Now, a baseball moving at 95 miles per hour is literally faster than the blink of an eye. If you blink at the wrong moment, you might never see it coming at all. But to this athlete, it looks enormous, like a pumpkin, because he's in a flow state and his focus is 100% on that ball. He's in this connected state of concentration and flow, where everything feels smooth and easy.

I asked him, "When you're in the flow, how's your breathing?"

He said, "It's relaxed, it's calm."

I reminded him about a game two weeks ago, when he didn't do very well. I asked how his breathing was then.

He said, "Oh man, I was agitated and tense. My breathing was erratic, really short, and choppy, and stressed."

So when this pro athlete is in the zone, his breathing is slow, relaxed, and effortless. Even when he's about to go up against that same pitcher who had his number two weeks ago, that didn't matter. In fact, nothing else mattered. Because he was in a flow state.

Another sign of a flow state is when you lose track of time. Have you ever been doing a task that you really enjoyed, or that was really engaging, and when you looked at the clock, you realized hours had passed without you realizing it? That's because you were in a flow state—your mind and body were connected as one. You were concentrated on the task at hand, and you were so immersed in that activity that you lost perception and sense.

Tell me, did time speed up in that two or three hours? No, but your level of interest and engagement in the activity or in the conversation was definitely piqued. You were present during that time. Your thoughts weren't too far ahead, and they weren't too far back.

I have a business partner, Mike Hatfield, who is a wonderful friend, a terrific colleague, and has a vast wealth of knowledge when it comes to mental skills training. Mike has almost ten years of experience in training US Special Forces with the Army, as well as working with professional athletes and collegiate sports. One of his favorite things to work on with athletes is concentration and breathing.

Mike likes to say that concentration is an endurance sport. He teaches it that way because he wants his students to understand that it's like anything else in sport: the more you practice, the better you're going to get.

Concentration is a skill, you can work on it, develop it and improve it. It's not set in stone. Who you are today does not mean that that is who you have to be tomorrow. You can be better than you were yesterday and that includes concentration!

Now, in the modern age, we have distractions everywhere. Our smartphones, with social media and push notifications, constantly pull our attention. Browsing online, we have pop-up ads, emails, and links to click. At school, we have other kids sitting around us, fidgeting, talking and playing with the stuff on their desk. Driving in the car, the radio is a distraction, and so are the other drivers, not to mention the other people in the car with you.

But we still have a choice. We choose what to focus on. That's why, if you're going to get better at concentration, you must think of it as an endurance sport (*thanks Mike*).

A common concentration thinking trap that athletes run into is to get distracted by, and become fixated on, an uncontrollable. Something like a bad pass, or a bad shot, or a bad referee or an umpire call.

Instantly, where has your concentration gone? You've taken it from the inside, from focusing internally on your attitude, concentration, and effort, to focusing on external things that you can't control. You can actually feel yourself transitioning into a feeling of control loss, of feeling powerless, not because you've actually lost any part of your ability, but because now you're only seeing those areas that you don't control.

In this thinking trap, athletes become fixated on trying to change those things that they can't. An athlete will even try to convince a referee that they're wrong, which we all know is a fool's errand. A referee may be wrong, and they can be proven wrong with video evidence, but I've never seen a referee change a call after making it just because in their heart they got it wrong and want to make things right.

As an athlete, we must understand and agree that a referee or umpire doesn't win or lose games. Players, athletes, teams and their opponents win or lose games.

Below are two mental skills to develop that will help you reverse and avoid this common thinking trap.

MENTAL SKILL #1: BE WHERE YOUR FEET ARE

This first skill is currently getting quite a buzz in the medical and mental health communities. It's called "mindfulness," it's a meditation technique, and it's supported by a lot of research. Recent studies show that mindfulness meditation can improve a variety of physical and mental health conditions.

Meditation? You may be thinking. *Really?*

Really.

Mindfulness is really just a focus on being present. If you're picturing sitting on a floor with your legs crossed, meditating for hours, that's certainly an option, but it's not what a mindfulness practice generally looks like. These days, mindfulness meditation is done with the help of apps, articles, and social media. There are a variety of free apps and websites offering guided meditation sessions, usually about 10–20 minutes long. There are websites and magazines with articles teaching you about quick mindfulness practices you can incorporate into their everyday life. There are practices you can do while you're walking, while you're eating, or before you go to sleep. There are 30-second breathing routines to help you quickly calm down when you need to. There are practices for working through anger, anxiety, interpersonal issues, or any other issue you might encounter in your daily life.

Chances are, you already do some amount of mindfulness on your own, without realizing it. If you like to stop and take a deep breath, in and out, before stepping on the court; if you enjoy using certain moments in your day to remind yourself to stay present; if you find that you don't like the mindset you get into when you're on your phone or the internet too much; then you've got a working understanding of the basics of mindfulness.

I like to think of mindfulness as being where your feet are. It's a skill that we can practice, and it helps us refocus our thoughts to reconnect to the task at hand.

MENTAL SKILL #2: THE RESET ROUTINE

Let me ask you something. How do you break a bad habit?

Consider some of the suggestions you might have, some of the techniques you've tried in the past.

Now, here's my answer.

To break a bad habit, you have to develop a new one, and you have to practice it, repetitively, consciously, on purpose. You have to practice it until it's instinctive, where you don't even have to think about it.

Take a simple bad habit, like nail biting. Let's unpack how many behaviors and practices are embedded within that one action.

First of all, nail biting is often a response to stress. When you're nervous or tense, it gives you something to do and helps you feel like you're in control. Nail-biters often find it satisfying to tear off their nails, strange as it might sound.

There's also a rhythm of biting that can feel calming on its own. Nail-biters often don't realize that they're chewing their nails unless someone else points it out; it's a soothing habit that becomes automatic and unconscious.

Then there's swearing. Did you know that studies show swearing can actually reduce the sensation of pain? That's why people swear when they stub their toes. (But it only works if you don't swear all the time.) We swear when we're frustrated, or angry, or just want to add emphasis to what we're saying. It becomes a substitute for expressing our emotions; we feel like we're venting, but we haven't actually talked about our emotions. Like nail-biting, swearing can become so automatic that we don't even think about it, and it gets hard to stop when we want to.

Similarly, negativity is a bad habit. Chronically negative people have become that way over time (because no one is born negative!) by surrounding themselves with other negative people, exposure to negative forms of content, speaking and acting negatively, day after day. And this habit gets reinforced by others. If you're a negative person, others tend to respond to you negatively, either by avoiding you or by supporting your negative talk, either of which will reinforce that behavior. If you're a positive person, people will be drawn to you and will speak more positively around you. Either way, whatever you put out into the world tends to be what you get back.

That's why to break a bad habit, you need to establish a new one, and not only that, you also need to build those supporting behaviors. If your friends smoke and you want to quit, limit spending time around them, or change your friend association completely. If you're going to change your negative behavior, you have to find positive things to focus on and talk about. Breaking one bad habit, if you do it successfully, can change your whole life. Once you've fixed that one habit, you tend to have a snowball effect where now you have the confidence and resources to make other changes in your life.

When it comes to concentration, your bad habit may be regularly checking out; checking your phone, looking around, chatting to someone else instead of listening intently or fidgeting instead of *staying where your feet* are and ***being present***.

MENTAL SKILL #3: PRACTICE PERSPECTIVE & QUIT COMPLAINING

One of the best ways to save yourself from the thinking trap of distraction is to practice perspective.

I often hear athletes around me complaining about the most trivial, minuscule things—someone's tone when they were talking to them, some tiny flaw in their equipment—and it hijacks their concentration. That negativity completely takes over, and they lose all focus.

What I do in these cases, and what an athlete can do for themselves, is to provide a little outside perspective, a little inspiration.

One of my favorite sources of inspiration is Nick Vujicic. He was born with a congenital condition called tetra-amelia syndrome, which means he has no arms and no legs. Nick is an Australian evangelist, a world-renowned speaker, with a beautiful wife and three kids. He drives a prototype vehicle that was developed for him, he's a talented swimmer, Nick has a blog, he's a best-selling author. Did you catch this…? **Nick has no arms, and no legs.**

His book, *Life Without Limits*, is a source of inspiration for myself and many athletes I've had read his books over the years. He has a beautiful positive perspective that we can all learn from; he's overcome such massive challenges. In *Life Without Limits*, he mentions that he was relentlessly bullied as a child, and was even suicidal at one point, but he didn't even have a way to commit suicide. Even if he were to try to drown himself in a pool, there were always lifeguards watching him because they knew how helpless he was. Imagine feeling so helpless and in such despair that you want to take your own life, but even worse than that, not being able to. Yet he overcame even that and went on to develop healthy relationships, and to become a world-renowned success story.

So when I hear my athletes griping about something tiny like their food or equipment, or their latest workout or warmup, or something someone said to them, I take them aside and tell them to check out one of Nick's videos. I'll say to them, "Look, no matter how bad you think it is right now, this video should change your perspective" That's how confident I am that Nick's work can change my athlete's mindset.

I'd like to challenge you to go take a look at one of Nick's videos online. Just start one and give him 5 minutes of your time. After 5 minutes, if you haven't had a shift in perspective, then you really need to recalibrate your attitude compass, because that man is an exceptional human being.

Nick had two options when he was growing up, and I see this all the time in athletes I work with who have medical limitations of any kind. Nick could have accepted his medical condition as the final word on his life. He could have accepted that he would always be dependent on others, could never achieve his dreams, that he would always feel lonely and helpless and that was just going to be his life.

But Nick didn't do that. Some of the best athletes make a similar choice that Nick did. They say, *OK, this is where I'm starting off. Maybe it's not great, perhaps I have some disadvantages. But I believe I can improve. I'm going to chase that and keep growing.*

In coaching and education, we call these two mindsets the "fixed mindset" and the "growth mindset." A fixed mindset is easily defeated because someone with this mindset thinks they are always going to have the level of skill and talent that they currently have—it will never get significantly better. This mindset sees any setback as proof that they can never get better.

You see this all the time in kids who struggle with math or science, and say, "I'm just not a math person." They look around at the kids doing better than them, and say, "They're just math people. They just get it. It's easy for them. I'll never be that good." What they don't see is the hours and hours of effort those other kids are putting in to get better at math.

A growth mindset says, *Wherever I am today, I can improve. I can get better, little by little if I try. I can get better at things I'm not very good at today, if I invest the time and effort, and try to think of new ways to improve and grow.* This mindset is tenacious and resilient. It tends to see setbacks as learning experiences.

I think it's obvious which mindset Nick has.

Which mindset do you have?

EFFORT

In Houston, where I live, we're close to the ocean. When you're out in the water up to your waist, you can see waves coming, six, eight, or ten feet taller than you. What do you do? You can stand where you are and probably get knocked over. You can take a step back. But the best way to handle the wave is to dive under it and come up on the other side. If you do that, you'll come out still standing tall, and you'll have moved forward out into the ocean. You took that wave quite literally, head on.

Adversity comes in waves, and it will hit you when you're not looking. When a wave hits, you have to decide if you're going to get out of the water or face the next one with whatever you've got. If you only have 20% of your average energy on a given day, that's what you offer. If you're injured, or tired, or facing a different challenge that day, you give 100% of what you've got.

Have you ever seen the ocean waves 100% completely stop? Life's waves come at you whether you're ready or not, they will never 100% completely stop. You decide what you are going to give.

Champions are not made on a calm, still day. They're made by encountering wave after wave, years of waves of adversity, and confronting them and fighting for air.

The thinking trap every athlete can relate to when it comes to effort is tricking yourself into thinking you're giving 100% when you're not. This happens when you're already tired or sore, often towards the end of a practice session. We let our level of effort slip and convince ourselves that it's not slipping, that we're still giving our 100%. We give ourselves permission, because we're tired or sore, to take it down a notch. We believe that we can't do our absolute best anymore because we're tired and sore, so our effort starts to slip. Belief becomes behavior, behavior becomes belief, and all of a sudden, we're slacking off a little bit because we felt, or rather decided, that we have to.

If I ask you to raise your arms to the ceiling at 70% effort, and if you have a sore shoulder, you may believe that you can't raise your arm as high as the others. You automatically give 60% to their

70%, perhaps without even trying to see what you, personally, can really do.

I want any athlete to understand that no matter how tired or sore you may feel, whatever the coach is asking you to do, you always have the capacity and ability to give 100% at whatever level you brought into that day. Your limit is not what you believe it is, or what you decide it is. Your limit is when you pass out, and if that happens, unless you have a medical condition, you'll come to.

That's not to say you need to push yourself to the point of hurting yourself and sustaining a lasting injury. It's to say that your mind doesn't get to decide, all by itself, what your 100% is. Your mind will always trick you into tapping out before you really need to. Your 100% is something that you choose, deliberately, by pushing yourself beyond the limits your mind wants to set.

Just like choosing where to put your focus instead of letting your mind wander off whenever it wants, you set your 100% limit by fighting past that 70% limit that your mind wants to place, by asking yourself to do more.

MENTAL SKILL #1: REMEMBER THE WHY

The key to pushing through a challenging moment is to remind yourself why you're there in the first place. Dig down, if nothing comes to mind right away, then find a good reason.

If you're really struggling to find a reason to do something, that's a cue to check in with yourself. Is your attitude where it should be? Is this something you really believe in?

In my private coaching practice, I personally use this acronym a lot, and I am aware of others that use it too: W.I.N. It stands for: What's Important Now?

You ask yourself this question to give yourself some motivation. If you can identify what's important and what matters about what you're doing, you will be primed to go attack that task and give it your best. It's a way of aligning your mind and your body. Your mind understands the "why," so that gives your body the fuel it needs in terms of energy and effort.

Another strategy if you're really struggling with that "why," is to ask yourself, why not? Why not do this? Are you afraid of pain, or rejection, or is it just that you don't want to do this? Once you have that answer, the "why not," you can face those issues.

MENTAL SKILL #2: SMALL GOALS FOR A BIG PLAN

When it comes to effort, we need to have the mental skill of setting goals according to a bigger plan. If you just set one huge goal that's unattainable or too far out of reach, it can really sap your motivation. It feels intimidating, it's too easy for your inner critic to say, *I'll never get there.*

It works much better to set smaller attainable goals, even daily ones, along the path that you'll need to follow to achieve your larger plan. These goals should be focused on effort, not necessarily outcome; they should be focused on things you can control. If you do set a goal for a non-controllable, you should have a few different ways of measuring success, whether it's a percentage, or a result, or a technique.

We do this for the same reason restaurants serve appetizers. You need something you can start with, something to entice you as you're getting started on this much bigger meal. You need to have something right in front of you, that you can reach, that's going to be appealing to reach for. That's the attainable goal—the small goal for that week or even that day. You can start on any plan, any seemingly audacious goal, by breaking it down into its smaller attainable goals. That way it becomes much more doable, and you gain motivation from knowing that your next goal is right in front of you and that it's very achievable.

It's important to be able to delay gratification, to sacrifice the immediate enjoyment of staying in bed or staying on your coach, and instead to go and work out, or go and do the task that you need to do. That's a useful skill. But it's also important to be realistic: sometimes you do need gratification. Small amounts of pleasure, to encourage you to keep going. Make yourself get up and go for that early morning run, then come home and reward yourself with a delicious breakfast. Don't say to yourself, *I'm going to take my ten-minute mile down to seven minutes, even if it takes me six months, and I'm not going to reward myself or have any kind of indulgence until I achieve that goal.* Six months is a long time to go with no rewards and no gratification, just saying.

What if, instead, you were to say, *I want to get my ten-minute mile down to seven minutes. For every 30 seconds that I get off my time, consistently, I'm going to give myself an extra rest day, or I'm going to enjoy a meal at my favorite restaurant, or I'm going to go on a day trip with my friends or family.* Even better would be to say, *I want to get my ten-minute mile down to seven minutes. To do that I think I will need to go for a run four mornings of the week for the next six months. For every week that I do all four sessions, I'll reward myself.* That way, you are setting a goal and rewarding yourself for something you are in control of—your effort.

Rewards are one kind of gratification, but another type that we don't always think of is the gratification of accomplishment. If you set attainable goals, smaller goals that can be achieved in a day or a week, that sets you up for that feeling of accomplishment. You'll feel like you did well—as if you're making progress—because you met your goal. That positive feeling, that gratification, rolls over when you're working on the next goal, and the next one.

I asked a room I was working with, "How many of you are 15 years old and older?" About a third of the room raised their hands. So I said, "If you have a two-day tournament on Saturday and Sunday, how many of you would go to the high school dance and stay out until 11 PM on Friday night?" Only a few hands went up.

I said, "Why not?" They said, "Well, we need our sleep, and we need to be ready for tomorrow."

I asked, "Am I telling you not to enjoy the dance?"

They said, "No. You said, 'stay out until 11.' We could come home earlier."

That's exactly it. This isn't about depriving yourself or living a life completely different than your friends. It's about looking at your long-term goals. It's about understanding that you can go to the dance, you just need the discipline to come home in time to sleep at a reasonable hour. You can enjoy the foods you like, you just need the discipline to consider, around game time, what's going to give you the best energy and the best endurance for your sport.

When you go to cook a meal, you don't just step into the kitchen and say, *Great, let's make a lamb roast.* You need to think about what you'd like to cook, get the ingredients and then follow a recipe, step-by-step, to create a well-prepared meal.

When it comes to cooking, we're used to the idea that there are steps you need to follow to get the end result you want. If you skip the salt, your dish will taste bland and flavorless. If you try to rush it, it won't cook properly. There's no getting around it, there's no negotiating, there's no trying harder next time. You really can't compromise with the basics of cooking: you do what you need to do, what the recipe calls for, or your dish will turn out badly. We all understand that.

Yet when it comes to making a great athlete, athletes try to skip steps, cut corners, avoid inconvenience, they try to compensate with something else, try to make up for it later.

If I'm working with a tennis player, and he tells me, "Coach, I'm giving 100% of myself out there on the court, I'm doing great," but I know that athlete loves to head back to the clubhouse after practice and order himself a big greasy Philly cheese steak sandwich and an ice cream sundae… may not agree that he's putting in the right kind of effort. He's focusing his effort where it's convenient for him, but he's skipping steps. Diet is crucial for an athlete. It's like the salt or the heat in cooking, you can't compromise on it. It's a non-negotiable.

After a practice, it's important for athletes to stretch before they go home. They tend not to like that. It's inconvenient—people feel they're done with the session and they want to leave. But it's what they need to do so their bodies can rest and begin to recover.

Likewise, I'll see an athlete leaving practice and eating a candy bar. Again, these athletes are looking at what's convenient, but they're skipping steps, or at the very least, missing opportunities. If my kids take the time to stretch, they'll perform better sustainably over time. If my hungry athlete eats real food with some protein and carbs after practice, his body will absorb more nutrients and recover better.

You as an athlete are trying to do something difficult: create a career from your talent and your skill. A great athlete is like a great dish; it has many components, and many steps go into making it, and each action has to be done correctly.

If you want to be a great player, don't complain when your coach is telling you that you need to give a better effort on the foot ladder drills because you're slacking off, you're not giving great energy and great effort towards hitting all the rungs of the ladder. But with a racket in your hand, you're an all-star. How difficult is it going to be to grow and to improve if you're only giving the effort when it's convenient, and only when you feel like it? The effort you need to give extends to every aspect of your athletic life.

I've worked with a lot of athletes and teams. Whenever I'm meeting a new group, I observe them carefully. I look at the details of their practices and games—their body language, how they carry themselves after a loss *and* after a win, how they walk onto their court or field and how they leave the field or court. With the high-performing athletes, I'm always interested to see what they're doing differently than the other kids.

At the junior level, most athletes seem to be doing things roughly the same. As they age, there are deviations that tend to snowball. You start to see that the elite athletes have put thought into every detail of their game, behaviors that aren't even on the other kids' radar. They're looking at extra reps, extra sprints, create extra opportunities for simulated competition in practice, they're stretching, focusing on hydration, diet, and even their sleep.

These elite athletes have all asked themselves the question at some point, *How bad do I want to be successful?* They've had a coach give them a tip, or they've heard about some new practice that another athlete is doing, and they've asked themselves, *How bad do I want it? Bad enough to try cutting down on my sugar intake? Bad enough to try tracking how much water I drink? Bad enough to go to sleep at the same time every night? Is that too much effort, or am I willing to do that?* And their answer is always, "Yes. I want it bad enough to pay attention to that tiny detail of my game.

THE GROUND RULES

1. Be prepared to re-evaluate old habits and assumptions.
2. Don't be afraid to disagree. Critical thinking is an important part of this process.
3. Be determined, patient and consistent; it may take time to see results once you start applying these concepts.
4. Maintain an open, teachable mind.
5. Empty your cup

COACHABILITY, EXECUTION AND AWARENESS

THE GROUND RULES

1. Be prepared to re-evaluate old habits and assumptions.
2. Don't be afraid to disagree. Critical thinking is an important part of this process.
3. Be determined, patient and consistent; it may take time to see results once you start applying these concepts.
4. Maintain an open, teachable mind.
5. Empty your cup

Read through these quotes and keep these in the back of your mind as you go, they are important concepts for this chapter.

AUTHENTICITY:

Authenticity is not something we have or don't have. It's a practice—a conscious choice of how we want to live.

Authenticity is a collection of choices that we have to make every day. It's about the choice to show up and be real. The choice to be honest. The choice to let our true selves be seen.
—Brene Brown, The Gifts of Imperfection

LIBERATION:

Then you will know the truth, and the truth will set you free.
—John 8:32

Have you ever built a house? Maybe with a school group, or a volunteer organization? Have you ever been to a build site? What about watching a home built on television?

To build a house, you have to use your imagination. For most of the project, the inside doesn't look like a house. Below are some images with framing done, some electrical work completed, and insulation installed. You can see the general outline of the rooms and layout, but you really don't know what you're looking at.

It's the same with an athlete. As you're starting to set up the framework for the kind of athlete you want to be—what your values and priorities are—there is still so much growth to do that you really have to use your imagination in the beginning, if you want to understand what it is that you're trying to build.

In the last chapter, we talked about the importance of a good foundation. Here's that ACE pyramid again:

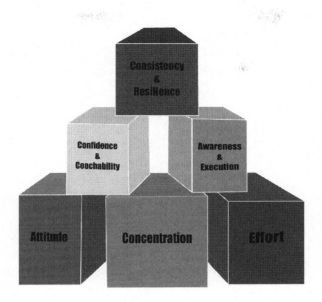

As you can see, the foundation of the pyramid is made up of the three ACE components: Attitude, Concentration, and Effort. In the example of building a house, these would be the solid foundation. In this chapter, I'll talk about those blocks on the second and third levels of the pyramid. Those are the components that are part of the structure of a good athlete: the walls that hold up no matter what kind of storm is raging outside, as long as you've got that good foundation.

COACHABILITY[1]

RELEVANCE TO ACE

Being coachable is a skill. You may have a natural gift for being coachable already, or it may be something you really need to work on, but either way, you can get better by putting in the time and effort.

---

[1] The coachability traits listed below are inspired by Human Kinetics (see resources list). I've made some minor modifications, but the foundation is theirs.

In other words, being coachable is within your circle of control. It's based on Attitude. Concentration and effort are still necessary, of course—you need to concentrate on your role or task, whatever it is that your coach is asking you to do. You also have to put in the effort to help your team and push forward the strategy your coach has given you, instead of just doing what you want.

A coachable athlete is a student of the sport. They're always looking for the next thing they can learn or improve. It doesn't have to be anything huge, just a tip picked up from another athlete or something you noticed other kids doing that you want to try in your next practice.

You just need to stay curious and open-minded about the game, always wondering if there's something else you could do better. You can learn from other athletes, both what not to do, and what to do. Either way, consider this—you're always learning.

Peyton Manning is one of my favorite examples of a coachable athlete. He retired in 2016, but he still holds the record for most career touchdown passes as of writing this (2019 with 539 career TD tosses). Manning who played 14 seasons as a quarterback for the Indianapolis Colts suffered a neck injury during a game in 2006, and the damage slowly got worse, caused more pain and weakness until finally, in 2010, Manning had to have surgery for a herniated disc. When he woke up, Manning's right arm and hand were weak. The disc had been pressing on a nerve, and there was nerve damage. Doctors didn't know if it would heal or not.

In the end, the Colts benched Manning for the 2011 season. He had a second neck surgery and then a third, a fusion surgery that involved soldering two of his vertebrae together. For the entire time he was out, Manning worked meticulously on improving his game, relearning his throwing action and rebuilding his strength bit by bit. He was so weak when he started rehabilitation that Manning could hardly flex his hand around the ball, so he focused on improving his grip strength.

That's the essence of coachability right there: learning to see the victory in tiny improvements and to keep working for the next development, even when your future is in doubt.

Manning essentially had to retrain his muscles to throw again, and because his arm strength never fully recovered, he had to relearn his game entirely to compensate for that weakness.

For 2012, the Colts had the first overall pick for the Draft. They released Manning and drafted Andrew Luck, a top-notch young talent. The Denver Broncos gave him a shot.

The remainder of Manning's career was just incredible. At 37, he was making significant improvements, reaching a better level of game than he ever had when he was younger and better than many athletes ever reach. He retired on a high note, after winning the Superbowl, at *39 years of age*.

Think about how his career could have gone otherwise. He could have insisted on fighting for his spot back with the Colts, pitting himself against Andrew Luck, a top young quarterback in his own right. He could have given up and accepted that he would never play football again. Instead, he did the hardest thing possible. He started over as a decorated NFL champion and learned the most basic movements all over again. Then, once he was on a new team, he had the humility and the adaptability to set up fresh chemistry with new players and learn different strategies. He essentially had two separate football careers. It doesn't get much more coachable than that.

Then there's Steph Curry.

I believe Steph Curry is one of the most transformational basketball players that we've seen in the last decade in the NBA. He's extended the shooting range so far back that he's a threat to make a three-pointer from a few steps inside half court. Curry is an unbelievable shooting guard, but the way he transformed the game is by *giving up his shots to another player* with an even better chance of making the basket. He's an MVP himself, and a game-changer in every sense of the word, but what's really special about him is that ability of his to focus on the bigger picture and see where his other teammates have a better chance.

Don't get me wrong, Curry can get up a shot whenever he wants or he is feeling on fire, but he's also got the team first mindset and gives people opportunities to shine.

Sacrificing for the team means following the game plan even if it determines that you, personally, don't look as good or score as many points. Think of it this way: if you have a great game and your team lost, how does it sound hearing a self-proclaimed star, on the losing side, bragging about their statistics while the team just lost.

Let's call it what it is. The arrogance look is not a good look, and it is very self-destructive to a team's chemistry and morale not to mention reputation.

This really comes down to identity: are you a team player, or aren't you? If you really don't feel you need to look out for your team, and you don't see how their long-term success matters more than how many points you score in one game, then you need to take a hard look in the mirror.

BE BETTER, NOT BITTER

A coach who recruited a young athlete playing college football, Adam, was replaced, and a new coach came in with new recruits and a new strategy. Adam didn't seem to fit in with their new plan. All of a sudden, he was being berated and beat up on by the coaching staff, to the point where he seriously considered just becoming a student and dropping out of the athletic program altogether.

In a situation like that, you have options. You can transfer schools, which is what Adam decided to do. However, he still had a few games left to play. My advice to him was, "For those last few games, forget the name-calling and just focus in on what they're telling you to do. Find what it is that they're telling you as a way to get better." A coachable athlete knows there is always a way to get better. It's just a question of finding it, even in a critical coach's hurtful words.

I can't take the credit for this saying, but I really like it: *Let the criticism make you better, not bitter.* If the coach stops talking to you, that's when you should really worry, because it could mean they're starting to give up on you. As long as they're still talking to you, even if they're being critical, they still believe in you, and you can still learn from it.

POSITIVE RESPONSE TO DISCIPLINE

Any coach can read a room, it's a big part of how we do our jobs. So when I'm handing out some discipline or laying down the law to my team(s), I'm observing their reactions very carefully. I can tell from the slope of a shoulder or the roll of an eye whether or not my athletes are absorbing what I'm saying or if they're blowing me off. They don't even need to be making eye contact for me to get a read on them.

As an athlete, you might be thinking, *But I didn't **say** anything. I'm entitled to my facial expression!* For sure! But your negative body language is information, it reveals a lot more to me about your attitude than you think.

Now, "discipline" in this section means criticism or feedback. It could be a specific instruction, like asking you to work on a particular technique for next practice, or just a constructive observation, like telling you your game is lacking in a specific aspect and you need to step it up. Any kind of correction or reproof. Your job as the athlete is to take that constructive criticism and try to figure out how to do what you've been asked—deliver that improvement or iron out that weakness.

ACCEPTANCE OF ROLE

When I say "role," I mean the role on a team—the position you play. You may not like the position you were given. Play it anyway. As we learned with ACE, you don't control the coach, and you don't control where they place you on the team. All you can control is what you bring to that role. Can you have a say in it? Set up a meeting or conversation with the coach and ask if you can share your feelings on the matter. Good chance, your coach will share back his / her feelings. Regardless, they're the coach, and you may be convincing. You may be not.

I'm a prime example of an athlete who did everything I was asked and still didn't earn the coaches' favor early in my college baseball career. But that's how it goes sometimes. With ACE, we don't follow the ego. Your ego will tell you that you need to be the best and have the highest status and anything less is unacceptable.

We're more interested in self-respect. Self-respect says, *This isn't the role I wanted, and I think I can do more. But I'm not the kind of person who lets something like this derail me. I'm still going to put in 100% of my effort while hoping and believing that something changes for the better.*

Being agreeable with the coach means adapting to their approach even when you don't like it or agree with it. I had to do this in high school—I was on an excellent basketball team, and we had the weapons to score. A lot. But a new coach came in who was all about defense. It was tough for us because under the new strategy we weren't scoring the same high points we were capable of, but we quickly realized that we had to adapt to our coach's agenda if we wanted playing time. So, we got on board and adopted the mindset that whatever the coach asked, we would do it. This comes back to the ACE mentality; we couldn't control the coach or the game strategy, we could only control ourselves.

The outcomes spoke highly. We became defensive machines and outworked our opponents on both ends of the floor. We played with high intensity, and a fierce competitive spirit. Regardless who was stepping into the gym to play us, we knew that we were bringing an intensity of ACE.

The sooner you can buy into the coach's plan, the quicker you can develop rapport and gain opportunities for you to add elements to their game plan. If you show resistance to the coach's approach, and let them see that you don't like it, most coaches will dig in their heels and insist on their approach until you fall in line.

It's easier and better for the team if you, as the athlete, put in the work to try to see where your coach is coming from and what the benefits of their plan are. Then you can genuinely follow along with their plan and start to build that crucial chemistry between the team and the coach.

Ultimately, there isn't just one way to win the game. There are hundreds of different strategies and combinations of tactics and talents that can win. So, the important thing is not trying to set the "right" strategy for the team; the important thing is that everyone is united, focused and throwing their energy behind the same goals. The trust that the athletes put into their coach is a crucial part of that. The most brilliant coach in the world won't win a single game if his team doesn't back or believe in him.

RESOURCES:

» http://www.humankinetics.com/all-coaching-and-officiating-articles/all-coaching-and-officiating-articles/finding-and-building-coachable-athletes
» https://canada.humankinetics.com/blogs/excerpt/being-coachable

EXECUTION

To be a mentally tough athlete and team, you need to be able to execute. You need to have mental reserves to call upon when it's time to push hard. You need to be able to put aside distractions and give maximum effort without hesitation. You need to get into a flow state where you feel calm and confident, and where everything flows timelessly around you—your breath, your teammates, the ball.

What if instead of feeling confident, you feel hesitant? That's likely because one of the primary ACE components is a little bit off, too. If you find yourself lacking confidence, it's a good time to stop and reflect on how your ACE is doing, because chances are, your attention has turned back to external things that are out of your control, and it's splitting your commitment. You're not living in that moment, passing the basketball or swinging the bat. Your mind is off worrying about the score or wondering what the other team is going to do.

Close your eyes for a moment and recall a time when you were playing with supreme confidence. I mean it—give it a try for a minute or two.

Really. Close your eyes. Re-live that moment.

•

•

•

•

•

Recalling that time, what were you seeing around you? When you're in that perfect mindset of just executing what's in front of you, there's no worry or fear. If you're playing baseball, you see the ball coming, and you hit it. If it's golf, you see the ball and the flagstick, you feel your shot, line it up, and just swing. If it's volleyball, you see the ball, get a sense for the other players, feel it, and decide to pass to your setter—all in an instant.

We're at our best as athletes when we're not thinking at all, when we're just executing. Many athletes describe that moment of being almost in slow motion. Executing starts with your mindset, not your surroundings. You have a positive and motivating mindset—you're not focused on the result—you're just seeing what you need to execute on in that moment.

An example of excellent execution is the unforgettable moment in basketball history when "His Airness" Michael Jordan jump shot in the closing moments of game 6, over Bryon Russell of the Utah Jazz, during the NBA finals in 1998.

Jordan's concentration was dialed into setting up a jump shot. He had a positive attitude and put in incredible effort to come up with that play in the final seconds of the game. His team was behind, with 60 seconds left in the game. Karl Malone was dribbling the ball at the baseline, and Jordan came around the corner, stole the ball, took it down to the other end of the court and set up his jump shot.

A moment like that is pure execution.

Nick Foles, with the Philadelphia Eagles, winning their first ever Super Bowl against Tom Brady and the Patriots (2018) is a more recent example of execution.

In his post-game interview, Nick Foles was asked, "How did you win?" His answer wasn't about any grand strategy, which you think they'd need to beat Tom Brady, the GOAT (greatest of all time). No,

Nick talked about the little things they did. Working on plays for weeks to make sure they could execute them, working together, keeping their confidence up, being aware that they didn't always look great during practice, but the Eagles were making the progress they needed to be making. The tiny details of the game. Execution starts with putting a process in place that you can trust to get you where you need to be.

HOW TO EXECUTE

When you're at your best, you don't think. You react, and your inner creativity explodes. By utilizing the ACE strategy, you maintain a position of readiness for "The Moment," or any situation that the game brings.

Have you ever wondered how some people can make unbelievable plays again and again throughout their careers? Part of it, I would argue, is that their ACE is locked in. When bad things happen, their attitude is like a knee-jerk reflex—they snap out of it and keep going, thinking about the next movement, the next play. They're self-correcting in the moment and getting their head back in the game.

When you're executing, you're fully dialed into your ACE. And when you're dialed into your ACE, your concentration is simple: **one thought, one focus, one task**. That frees you up to be the best athlete you can be, simply because you can focus your whole being on just one moment, *one execution*. And ultimately, that's where true confidence comes from. Confidence is diving into something, really committing, knowing that everything else will take care of itself. ACE is a strong way to help you get there.

Some people refer to executing as "rising to the occasion." A challenge comes up, and you rise to overcome it. But I don't really see it that way.

Many people will tell our military veterans that they're heroes (including myself) thanking them for their service and sacrifices, but a Navy Special Operator once shared with me the way SEALs think about rising to the occasion.

He said, "Our belief is, we don't *rise* to the occasion, we **fall back** on our training."

He went on, "When somebody is a hero on our team, when someone tries to rise to the occasion and do something extraordinary, bad things happen, and people die, because being a hero to me means going beyond what you think is possible instead of sticking to the plan. Instead, we have the mindset that you don't have to be extraordinary to be great at your job."

I really like that approach. How many times have you heard a coach, or a motivational speaker say, "Let's go!! We've got to rise to the occasion!"? It's a dangerous philosophy because it means there's a challenge and you're sending your team out there with the feeling that they need to put on their superman cape.

We have a tendency then to try harder to pull off some sort of Superhuman feat. It sounds good, but it's not likely to happen. The SEAL philosophy is, your training should have prepared you for this, and you should know what your job is and how to do it. If you just do your job, you'll do great.

That's what execution is about. It's about preparing and practicing so that when the moment comes, you can be calm and confident and just feel like you're doing your job. No superhuman feats. No once-in-a-lifetime shots. Just the same things you do every day.

AWARENESS

Awareness is an action. It might *sound* like a state of mind, something passive that you either have or you don't have. But when it comes to humans, because of our busy minds, awareness is something you have to do. Crucially, it's the *first* thing you have to do if you want to improve anything about your life.

My pastor said it best: "When it comes to self-improvement or getting better at anything, you first have to take a critical, honest look in the mirror. You have to raise your self-awareness and ask yourself, *Where am I at right now?*"

Awareness is essential in change management—a discipline that businesses use to understand where they are right now, where they're headed, and where they want to be. It's referred to as *current state* and *future state*. Current state is where you are right now. Future state is where you want to be.

When companies look at their current state, they have to assess themselves very objectively. Let's say a company wants to figure out what its corporate culture is like—how people tend to act and treat each other in the company. They'll survey employees, or pay consultants to come in and run focus groups or a top-down review because they need to know exactly where they're at right now if they want to plan to make changes. They want the plain, unvarnished truth.

This concept is beginning to make its way into sports as I write, but hasn't been fully adopted mainstream yet. When I run ACE seminars with groups of athletes, I'll occasionally find an athlete who tells me everything is great. Their attitude is great, their concentration is great, their effort is great. So I'll ask a few more questions: "Is there any area of the game where you could improve?" Some will name a few things they feel they could improve. Others will say, "You know, I don't think so."

I'll ask, "Even if I bring your coach in, your coach will say there's nothing you need to improve?" "I really can't think of much." Well, considering that world-class athletes are continually improving their game, I'm always a little skeptical whenever I meet someone who really doesn't see any need to improve. What that tells me is that athlete lacks awareness, and it could be a significant blind spot that is holding them back.

Awareness comes back to Ground Rules #4 and #5: "Be honest and open," and "Empty your cup." Being aware is about being authentic.

Authenticity is not something we have or don't have. It's a practice—a conscious choice of how we want to live.

> **Authenticity is a collection of choices that we have to make every day. It's about the choice to show up and be real. The choice to be honest. The choice to let our true selves be seen.**
> **—Brene Brown, *The Gifts of Imperfection***

Authenticity is about letting our true selves be seen. Seen by our loved ones, recognized by our coaches, and everyone we're trying to work with or impress. Seen by ourselves.

This doesn't mean we wall ourselves off and dismiss everyone else's opinion because "they don't understand the *real* me." Quite the opposite—we allow ourselves to be seen by others, and we value the feedback that we receive. We know there's something true in it somewhere. When you're being authentic, and you know others are seeing you as you really are, it's hard to dismiss their opinions.

A lot of times, our friends and family see us more accurately than we see ourselves. Our friends and family can usually tell when we're upset or stressed, no matter how well we think we're hiding it. So to build your awareness of yourself, and therefore your authenticity, incorporate some of the feedback you're getting from other people. If everyone sees you a certain way, even if it's different from how you see yourself, sometimes there's some truth to it.

A young athlete at a sports academy, Dan, had come to the US from another country. He worked with us for his post-graduate year (graduated high school and utilized a gap year to be better prepared for college), and he grew by leaps and bounds; literally, he put on 25lbs over the year. But he was still just 5"8 and only 145 lbs by the end of the year, and his game wasn't perfect. He started to make shots, even three-pointers, but he still lacked confidence in his ability to dribble and see the plays happening before they did. Even so, he got offered an NAIA Division I junior varsity spot, which was amazing to me.

But as Dan was talking to the coach about the opportunity, the coach started saying something that this young athlete didn't really like hearing. He said, "I love your energy and all of the elements you're going to bring to this team that aren't athletic. You're bringing heart, you're bringing passion, you're bringing energy, you're bringing character, you're bringing integrity, you're bringing academics and discipline." The coach went on and on, naming all of these intangible elements that he was really excited to get in this athlete. "If I could combine my best players' athleticism with your components, we would be playing for titles this year."

I heard it from Dan himself when he came back from talking to the coach. He shared this conversation with myself and the other coaches, and you could see the sadness on his face. So I asked him, "Dan, why the long face? I've worked with some of the best athletes in their respective sports, and I've never heard a coach talk about a young man like this. You've earned this coach's respect, and you haven't even played for him yet. That's incredible, and you should be proud of yourself!"

Still sad and dejected, Dan said, "Yeah, but it's junior varsity. And not even NCAA; it's NAIA, it's a lesser division."

I said, "But look where you came from. You came from another country, no American college would consider you right out of high school because of your height and your ability at the time. You worked your way up this whole year at the academy, and now you've been given a jersey spot. I know you had bigger goals, but man, you shot for the stars and you landed on the moon." I held up my hand for a high five.

Dan just looked at my hand, and let his face sink a little more.

"No high five? No love?" I asked.

"I just wanted more..." said Dan.

My heart broke for the kid. I could only imagine how he was feeling. But the truth was, Dan's dream of playing college basketball was always a stretch. Someone of his size would have to be a one-in-a-million athlete just to be considered, and his game wasn't at that level. I don't know how it happened that he made it that far without realizing the truth—whether someone lied to him, or he just got caught up in the social media hype. Whatever it was, Dan wasn't seeing himself clearly.

In the end, he was so discouraged he didn't even take the junior varsity offer. He returned to his home country, completed university and is a basketball coach now. There's nothing wrong with that. But he was clinging to the dream of big-time Division I NCAA college basketball, and when he didn't get it, he was just devastated. It didn't need to be that hard on him. At any point, Dan could have taken a hard look at his stats and attributes, and compared them with the people he knew who succeeded. He could have decided that he loved playing basketball, but maybe he wasn't going to be an NCAA Division I star, and that was okay.

The truth is, being fully self-aware, being authentic is hard. Taking that long look in the mirror can be hard if you're distracted by visions of who you want to be and who you could be, instead of just looking at who you are. That's where friends, family, and experts like coaches come in. They're often the ones who tell us when we're being unrealistic, whether we've inflated our abilities, or on the other end of the scale, dismissed our real gifts, unable to see their value.

When the people who care about you tell you something, it's worth listening, even if it hurts. When I told Dan that the junior varsity spot was actually a terrific offer based on his ability with the potential to earn a spot on the varsity team for years to come, that hurt for him to hear. But if he had listened, and taken the place, who knows how far he could have gone. Maybe he would have eventually proven that coach and me wrong!

PAYING ATTENTION TO THE GAME

Paying attention to the game is a key aspect of awareness. You need to be able to *feel* when the team is off. I've worked with teams and athletes who struggle with this—instead of feeling the game out for themselves and knowing instinctively where to go with the ball and who's got the hot hand (basketball) or who's the hot hitter (volleyball) right now, they rely on statistics or the coaches to tell them that. It holds their game and potential back.

If you're struggling to pay attention to the game, my recommendation is to channel your focus into just one aspect of ACE. Pick one and dial into it 100%. It will help narrow your focus, which will allow you to direct your energy where it's needed the most.

Imagine you're a Division III soccer player, and you've missed two or three open opportunities to put a ball in the net. You know your awareness isn't where it should be, and you can tell your attitude stinks right now, so you dial into it. You set everything else aside and give yourself permission to just think about one thing: the attitude you're carrying.

How do you know which ACE component to pick? My tip is, choose the one that's screaming at you the loudest. The one that manages to get your attention even during a game because it's so far off. Where the worst one is, the other two aren't far behind, so if you can improve the worst one, the others will also follow.

It's like a rope with three strands. If one of those strands starts to unravel, you can still pull weight on the rope. If two start to unravel, it's weaker but you can still pull something on the other end. It's the same with ACE. If you just have one good strand, say your Concentration is really good, you can still pull the other two along with you, but it'll put more stress on the rope as long as it's in that unravelled state. What you really need is to bring in those other two elements and weave that rope back together.

This is something you'll get better at the more you practice and use ACE. You'll develop a sense for what components are off at any particular moment, and you'll be able to adapt and shift your attention to bring that component back in line. You'll become very sensitive to your attitude, concentration, and effort, and will start picking up on low points (where one of them is not doing very well), and high points (where one of them is doing great), that you never used to notice. It will become more and more instinctive and a natural part of your game, and it will help you come to understand yourself as an athlete in ways you never imagined.

Coaches teach us about awareness all the time, but it's our job as an athlete to be aware of the changing variables and the shifting environment of the game, and to prepare so that we can do something about it.

» Awareness in a team sport might look like:
» Being aware of the ball
» Sensing the other players
» Watching for offsides, plays, defenders, set plays
» Being able to still listen to the goalie, captains, and/or midfielders
» Communicating with the team and calling out what's happening with the ball
» Keeping your head on a swivel, to constantly take in the game

Depending on your position, most of the game may be happening in front of you or behind you, so awareness means keeping track of the space around you and being able to imagine where the next play will come from.

In baseball, as with soccer, awareness can be about sensing the next play and deciding what you'll do if that play starts to happen. For me as a baseball player, I used to play center field, I might be thinking to myself: *Okay, I have a guy on second and third base, one out, a fly ball short in front of me, I'll catch it and get ready to throw that guy out at home if he tags up and tries to score.*

As you can see, awareness in a baseball player might look like thinking two, three or even four plays ahead of the guy that's coming up to the plate.

If that fly ball happens, I'm ready; I catch the ball and throw him out at home, or if it's a deep fly ball, my only throw may be to third base… or ground ball base hit to me, I need to field it clean and come up ready listening for my infielders telling me to throw it home or to hit my cut off.

A young athlete who just turned pro out of high school, Jane, was exceptionally skilled at golf. There's a lower pro tour she entered into to earn her stripes and gain confidence before going to Qualifying School (Q School) to earn her LPGA Tour Card. When you're playing on tour, you're training and playing for your job and all hours of the day. On this tour, Jane had to play in the early morning. It was a huge shift for her because she spent most of her practice time in the late afternoon, after she would get out of school.

You might be wondering why the time of day makes such a difference. Well, golf is played outdoors, and it's played on grass, but unlike soccer, for example, golf is a game where victory is determined in millimeters. Throughout a day, the course conditions change, and the greens roll different sometimes from the morning compared to the afternoon. So, if you're used to playing in the afternoon and suddenly you start playing in the morning, the dew and condensation are a nice wake-up call which you may not have encountered very often.

Because of all of this, Jane's putts weren't going exactly where she wanted them to, typically rolling putts well through a hole or well short. But she figured out the solution for herself. She told me: "I need to be a lot more aware of the course, the surroundings, and all of the different variables at play. Not to mention, I do a good job of keeping track of the wind, Trevor, but the course conditions are changing throughout the day and week of the tournament. I need to be better prepared for that."

Jane saw the need for increased awareness, all on her own. That's one way to improve your external awareness when you play golf: tracking outdoor conditions and taking careful note of the changing conditions of the field.

Practice it! Seriously, practice awareness by:

» **Listening:** really listening, authentically, objectively and without your ego. That is to say, empty your cup.

» **Observing your senses:** be mindful and notice new things around you.

» **Asking for feedback from coaches, parents, and peers— beware in advance:** you may get some tough information in return...

A note on Point 3 in that list: getting feedback can be hard, especially if it's negative. The key is to be as authentic as possible, with yourself or others. If you're already seeing your mistakes and weaknesses and allowing others to see them, then there's no surprise when negative feedback comes through—it'll just reinforce something you already know, rather than coming out of nowhere and shattering your emotions. Even if it's feedback that seems way off, you can still ask yourself, "How can this help me? What can I get out of this that I can apply to my game and see an improvement?"

RELEVANCE TO ACE

Awareness requires Attitude to re-focus on taking criticism and opportunities to be better (not bitter), Concentration for your ability to lock into being more aware, and Effort to change habits.

To return to my baseball example from earlier, let's say I caught that flyball and I'm winding up to throw that guy out at home. I don't control the outcome of that throw. With ACE, I know that, and I can put it out of my mind.

Instead of worrying and thinking, *Am I going to get that guy out? I'm thinking, Track the ball, line up my throw, pro-hop through the ball, and aim to throw it 1 foot over my cut off man's head.* I'm focused on my technique, not the outcome, and my awareness is focused on all those tiny physical adjustments I need to make to perfect that throw in the moment. My mind and body are engaged with me, in that moment of making the throw, with that simple goal of catching it, transferring it in my glove, positioning my body, and throwing the ball.

Because ACE has directed my attention away from all of those distracting factors and worries, I have my awareness exactly where it will do the most good: on my physical performance in that instant. I'm liberated from having my focus pulled in a million different directions.

What does liberation feel like?

Jesus told his disciples, "*If you hold on to my teaching, you are really my disciples. Then you will know the truth, and the truth will set you free.*" (NIV).

Jesus was talking about a more profound spiritual truth, not necessarily sports. But we can apply this idea throughout our lives. The idea that the truth can set you free is a simple but powerful statement. In fact, many people instinctively hide from the truth. They don't think it will set them free; they believe it will hurt.

But when you know the truth, there are no more distractions or questions in your mind. You're able to focus single-mindedly on what's in front of you.

That's the kind of liberation I'm describing here—the freedom of knowing what matters, and letting go of everything that doesn't.

ACE doesn't guarantee you results, but it will ensure that you can be prepared when you need to.

THE GROUND RULES

1. Be prepared to re-evaluate old habits and assumptions.
2. Don't be afraid to disagree. Critical thinking is an important part of this process.

3. Be determined, patient and consistent; it may take time to see results once you start applying these concepts.
4. Maintain an open, teachable mind.
5. Empty your cup.

In the next chapter, we'll focus on confidence. We know it's not just about strutting and demanding attention. But lots of people still demonstrate confidence that way. I'm going to tell you that confidence is not the same thing as having a big ego. You might disagree with me, but remember Rule #2 and hear me out anyway.

EIGHT (B)

CONFIDENCE

THE GROUND RULES

1. Be prepared to re-evaluate old habits and assumptions.
2. Don't be afraid to disagree. Critical thinking is an important part of this process.
3. Be determined, patient and consistent; it may take time to see results once you start applying these concepts.
4. Maintain an open, teachable mind.
5. Empty your cup.

Confidence is one of the most important and elusive traits of an elite athlete, but it's something that most athletes don't know much about. Some use rituals and superstition to make themselves feel confident. Others mistake confidence for cockiness. In this chapter, I'll explain what confidence looks like for an ACE athlete and how to make sure you can be confident when you need to be.

CONFIDENCE

If you're an athlete or coach, chances are you've heard at some point that confidence is everything. You turn on ESPN Sports Center and in a 30-minute program, you may hear the word "confidence" a dozen times.

"He looked really confident out there today!"

"Boy, the team is lacking some confidence on the floor."

"That coach demands confidence!"

On Monday Night Football, ESPN has a segment called "You Got Mossed," after their NFL analyst, Randy Moss, a famous NFL Hall of Famer who played as a wide receiver. The segment shows a highlight reel of amazing catches, incredible feats that athletes have pulled off within recent games from high school, collegiate, and professional football. Even in that segment, the I've heard Randy's co-hosts say before, "Can you imagine the confidence of that guy, after he gets up from making a catch like that?"

Many athletes believe that if they're not confident, they won't play well. They think that confidence level is some magical indicator of performance, and worse, they believe it's not entirely under their control.

As a mental coach, I don't know that I would say confidence is *everything*. With the ACE method, if your confidence isn't at a reasonable level, you can work on it and improve it. I believe it's under your control to a degree, as it originates from your attitude and your concentration.

In saying that, just because you *are* confident, doesn't mean you've got your ACE sorted. When I peel back the layers of an un-confident athlete, I'm just as likely to find issues with the ACE components as with an over-confident athlete. A confident athlete can still have a crappy attitude. Their focus might be on the results and the outcome instead of their attitude, concentration, and effort.

Building a mentally tough athlete is like building a house. The components support and reinforce one another, good or bad. Confidence is a *result* of the three ACE components, as you can see from the pyramid diagram from the beginning of this chapter, but it also *affects* those components. So much of ACE is about perspective, and that goes for confidence too. What lens are you using to view your successes, failures, and overall performance?

I created a formula years ago with the help of an intern to visually demonstrate where confidence comes from. Here it is:

$$P^2 \times SB \pm E = C$$

The formula looks confusing. And it's intended to appear complicated because confidence can be. I aim to simplify it.

P = Past Performance
P = Preparation
S = Self-talk
B = Body language
E = Environment
C = Confidence

Simple, right?

An athlete could use this formula to "calculate" their confidence by reviewing each of the variables and inserting a certain amount, based on how well they're doing. So let's imagine an athlete, Sam, tallying up her confidence level going into an upcoming game.

The first variable is past performance. Sam's been doing great, so we'll consider that variable maxed out. Next is preparation. Sam's practices have been okay, not great. So we'll consider that variable at half strength. Next is self-talk. Well, since Sam's preparation hasn't been good, the self-talk hasn't been good either. So we'll consider those two variables are about the same. Then there's body language. Again, Sam's preparation and self-talk have both been lackluster, so the body language isn't very good.

Finally, we come to Sam's environment. Our conversation: "Sam, you're playing your biggest arch-rival in their home stadium. What's that stadium like to you? How does it feel when you walk in?" Sam might reply, "It's a little scary; the crowd gets really loud, and in the student section they heckle and boo." So right away, I there's a good chance that Sam's perspective could be negatively influenced in this environment.

I wouldn't usually let an athlete get away with saying that an environment is scary and therefore they're going to let it affect their game. That's not what ACE is about. Regardless of the venue, the actual court or field will always be the same, and the athlete can focus their attitude, concentration, and effort on that space rather than letting the crowd define that space for them.

In the film *Hoosiers*, there's a famous speech where the small-town team arrives at the big arena for the state championship. The coach (played by Gene Hackman) can see his team is a little overwhelmed, so he has them measure the height of the basketball net. "I think you'll find it's the exact same measurements as our gym back in Hickory, Indiana," he says, to chuckles from the team.

The court is always the same. It doesn't matter how hostile the environment seems; noise is noise, and it can be tuned out. It comes back to attitude and perspective; are you going to let yourself be influenced by hecklers and the environment, or not?

Returning to the equation, I like to present this to groups and ask them to pick out what the different elements mean. No one has ever guessed all of the variables right, because a formula like that is meant to look intimidating. It's intended to show how much we can overcomplicate confidence.

But confidence is simple, it's a result of having strong ACE. The five variables in the formula are real things that are helpful for athletes to consider, but like everything else I've discussed in this book, the foundation is ACE.

We covered awareness in the last chapter because to find your confidence, you need awareness first. You need to be able to tell when one or more of these 5 variables is off. You need to be able to ask yourself about each of them: *Is my preparation solid? How about my self-talk? What about my body language?* And you need to be able to answer yourself honestly: *You know what, my body language really isn't that strong. I wonder why? Maybe there's a disconnect between my self-talk and what my body is saying. How can I get my body and mind to be aligned? Perhaps I can try concentrating on a positive affirmation, something that really strikes home with me, and it'll help get my body language on track.*

It's a self-diagnostic tool—only you can run it, and it only works when you're being honest with yourself, and when you're authentic enough that you can acknowledge when something is wrong.

What do I mean by being authentic enough to acknowledge when something is wrong? Surely, athletes know when something's wrong? Yes, but like everything else, awareness is a skill, and you can get better at it. Knowing something's wrong is one thing. Figuring out what it is, and fixing it is something else.

Imagine that you're a basketball player, and you're struggling with your shooting in the first quarter of a game. Coming off the court, what do you think you'll be saying to yourself?

Why am I playing so bad right now? Why is my shot off?

Now imagine I'm standing there beside you. I'll start asking you those same questions you're asking yourself, but I'll take you through the five variables.

"When you were preparing before the game, how was your attitude?"

You'll say, "Great!"

I'll dig a little deeper, moving on to concentration.

"What were you focused on?"

You might say, "Well, I was focused on my release and getting my shot off quick."

Now, I'll ask the critical question: "And what's happening on the court this second?"

You'll say, "I guess I'm not releasing well and I'm not getting my shot off quick."

So now you, the basketball player, have found two simple things you can focus on right now: release and getting a quick shot. You may not be able to turn it around, you may still miss shots, but just believe that if you keep your focus on one or two things that you *can* control, good things will come from it.

If you go back out on that court with that mindset, in my experience, you'll see an immediate difference. You chose what to concentrate on, to improve your confidence. Maybe there are other things you could have focused on, maybe four or five or more things are going on, maybe next time you'll choose different things to look at, but the key is that you made a choice. You narrowed your focus to one or two things that you could remember and concentrate on effectively.

Now, you don't need a Trevor beside you at all times. This is something you can learn to do for yourself!

PREPARE!

If preparation is lacking, then you need to change your attitude and your concentration when it comes to those "bad practices." Does one lousy practice mean that you're not going to play well on Friday? No, it doesn't. What about effort? A bad practice yesterday doesn't necessarily mean a bad practice today. Dial into your effort and give everything you have, regardless of what happened yesterday.

An athlete can do this with each of the five variables—they all tie back to the ACE components in one way or another. For example, if your body language is off, you can ask yourself, *How is my attitude? It's awful because the coach just pulled me out of practice because I wasn't doing what I was supposed to. Okay, that's where my crappy body language is coming from.* So, I need to work on that attitude. You identify the weak point, trace it back to the ACE component(s) it's related to, and identify a way to improve it.

This doesn't have to be difficult or intimidating. It might sound complicated right now because I'm describing it as a step-by-step process. But it will quickly feel easy and natural once you've practiced it a few times. It'll become second nature, just like adjusting your stance before taking a shot or stretching out your muscles before a warmup.

Negative self-talk can put a big dent in your confidence. When you miss a few shots in a game, do you instantly become your own worst enemy? Think back to the Circle of Control. How is self-talk related to ACE? Well, it's rooted in attitude. So when you find yourself indulging in negative self-talk, focus on your attitude. See if you can change the negative self-talk to positive self-talk by adjusting your attitude.

Having confidence just means taking steps to be ready for whatever you're about to do, being prepared. If you feel ready, you'll have the confidence. If you know that your preparation is lacking, then the solution is obvious: prepare more. It really is that simple. When you've addressed that shortcoming, you'll see and feel your inner confidence coming through.

The more you practice ACE, the more it will become part of you. This book can introduce you to the concepts and the first steps you can take, but most athletes will take ACE much further in their own game. There's a certain amount of work that you have to do to pick this concept up and run with it, and you'll end up with a practice that's very customized to your sport and your abilities as an athlete.

I introduced the ACE method to a college football player, Phil. Phil ran with it to the point that it transformed his entire perspective on life, and he became one of the most positive individuals I've ever known.

When I was working with Phil years ago, everyone was wearing these rubber LiveStrong bracelets on their wrists. So I told Phil, "Every time your attitude goes south, you have to be aware of it. Snap your wrist once with the bracelet, and that will be your reminder to check in on your ACE and pick a component to dial into. Do something about that attitude by choosing a positive thought or action. Something, anything."

Several months later, Phil did something that **I am not advocating for anyone reading this book to do**, but I am sharing it as an example of how far ACE can take you.

Phil got an ACE *tattoo*.

It was a small circle on the inside of his wrist, right where he used to snap himself with the bracelet, with "ACE" inside the circle. Again, **I am not saying that anyone needs to go out and do that.** At all. I just want to illustrate how much ACE can become a part of your life, a practice that supports you and helps you attain the life you want.

In fact, Phil is not working in sports right now. He actually works in banking. He's taken that drive and positivity into a completely different industry, and he's using it to fuel his growth in an entirely different arena. I taught him ACE to make him a better athlete. I knew it had more potential than that, but he was a college football athlete at the time, so that's how I introduced it to him. It ended up transforming his entire life, and now he's truly happy in a new field.

(True story, but as I was writing this portion of the book, I reached out to Phil, and asked him if he still looks at his ACE tattoo and if he has any regrets of getting it. His response, "Every day I look at it, and I've never regretted it. It changed my entire perspective on life.")

EXAMPLES OF A CONFIDENT ATHLETE

When I say that a confident athlete looks the part, I'm not talking about being cocky and strutting around demanding attention.

Tony Robbins talks about aligning your mind and body. He uses the example of emotions and facial expressions, saying, "I'm happy, I'm happy," while his facial expression is actually showing anger and frustration. Would you believe that he actually is happy? Absolutely not. So why do we play that game with ourselves in our own head? Our internal message needs to match our physiology, whether it's our facial expression, our posture or the way we walk.

Here's an example of how this would look in an athlete.

A volleyball player, Ashley, just served into the net and she's getting crushed. On the inside, Ashley is trying to be positive. She's telling herself, *Let's go. Let's go. I have to do this. I have to keep going.* But her body language is exhausted, loose and sloppy. She's slumping over and looking down. You can see on her face how tired and frustrated she is. Ashley's too disheartened by the game to pay attention to her body language, but her teammates and coach can tell she's not in a good place. She is really trying, but she's clearly not playing at her best. Why not? One factor, at least, is that she isn't allowing her body to match her positive self-talk.

If Ashley has been taught the ACE method and practiced it, within a few seconds she'd clue in. She'd realize her body isn't matching her self-talk and she'll dial into her attitude. Pretty soon you'll see her rolling her shoulders back, standing up tall, taking some deep breaths. Maybe she'll do a Wonder Woman pose, with her hands on her hips, to give herself some confidence. Then that positive self-talk she's been trying to use will actually help, and she'll start calling out to her teammates, getting everyone back on track. Pretty soon the whole team is back in the game.

It is that simple and it can be that fast. Confidence is not some mysterious spirit that comes and goes, and no one knows why. It's something you can learn to be better at controlling.

If you want to be confident, convey confidence. Carry yourself with confidence. Roll your shoulders back, raise your chin so that your head is up, don't be afraid to take up space.

REFLECT ON PAST PERFORMANCES

The reason my confidence formula included "± Environment" is that:
1. It's fun—how often do you get to use that symbol?!
2. Adds a sense of curiosity and thinking for individuals seeing it
3. Environment comes down to an individual's perspective

It's "plus/minus" because your view of the environment changes. If you're playing to a packed house in your home stadium, it's easier to feel excited and confident. That could be considered a "plus" environment.

If you're going into hostile territory, packed with fans of the rival team, with everyone wearing the opposing colors, holding signs, and shouting profanities at your team, that can be a very different feeling.

But the real reason for the plus/minus is that you get to *choose*. There's the potential for good or bad, but when you're an ACE athlete, you can control your perspective. Any environment that you step into can give you a boost because it's where you're going to play your sport. The rules and dimensions of the sport doesn't change.

An ACE athlete isn't swayed by the change in scenery. Screaming fans don't change how you execute from play to play. Because you're prepared. You practiced. Your self-talk is great, and you've got the body language to match. ACE athletes recognize the environment for what it is and focus on what they have to do to execute their strategy, their skills, and do so with confidence.

ACE athletes also don't blame the environment. They don't say, "We lost confidence because it was a hostile environment and that's why we lost the game." Mentally soft players do that, and to me that excuse is not acceptable. You can choose your "A" going into any environment and view it as an opportunity to perform. The louder it gets, the more energized you should be, regardless of what they're screaming about exactly.

I love seeing coaches and athletes who walk into a hostile arena with smiles on their faces. Not a cocky, defensive smile, but a genuine, relaxed smile. You almost can feel like they're thinking, *This is what we play for. This is fun. This is exciting.*

How confident do those teams look?

That hostile environment is what you signed up for as an athlete. It's your workplace, and you've got to have the mindset and belief that you're good at your job. You know how to dial into your concentration, focus on what you can control and what you need to do, and just play the game.

Not that it isn't a struggle at times.

When I was on a high school basketball team, we were doing really well and playing in front of some pretty hostile crowds. For this one game, we were playing at a school where the student section was known for heckling the rival teams. They were very good at it. We all knew they would try to mess with us when we got there.

Sure enough, even as we were starting to warm up, the student section got going on us. They did their best to unnerve us. "Hey #10... you piece of *#*ja;3, why don't you just *3qj3&#^##!...(that's the PG version mind you)." Among many other hurled insults, I kept a relaxed smile on my face the whole time and just kept thinking, *It doesn't matter what you say to me. You're not playing this game.*

The very first play of the game, I gave a pass to one of our best shooters, and he sunk a three pointer from NBA range. As we're jogging back to the other side of the court, I made eye contact with one of the student hecklers who had been giving me personally so much crap. I winked at him. I wouldn't do this kind of thing now, of course—I wasn't the calm, collected, and calculated adult I am now. Well, at least that's my excuse.

After that, any time I touched the ball, I was public enemy #1, but it didn't matter. I was committed the game was going to be played within the lines, and we knew that, as a team, so we were unshakeable.

To caution the reader, winking at the crowd is not a good move. That kind of gesture feels powerful at the time, but you're still buying into their game, and your concentration now isn't on yours (even for a second). You're still acknowledging their importance and bringing them onto the court with you.

Again, it pulls your own attention from where it needs to be: the game. Really, if you let yourself be provoked like that, you've got some work to do as an athlete, and I can cheerfully acknowledge that I still had some work to do. But I will say, I caught myself. For the rest of the game, I didn't look at them again. I made my choice about what to concentrate on, and I stuck to it after that.

RELEVANCE TO ACE

You've heard coaches say for years, "Practice makes perfect," and then they changed it to "*Perfect* practice makes perfect." But if you're an accomplished athlete, you know: you're never perfect. There's always something else to work on. Something can always get better.

My philosophy is that practice makes permanent, and that creates habits. Habits and that state of "permanence" lead to the product on the field/court. So, as you're practicing, if you allow yourself to have poor effort or bad concentration, you're reinforcing those shortcomings every time you practice. When it is game time, you'll need to step it up. But we already said that "stepping it up" is not what you want. You don't want your best effort to be some rare, extraordinary event. Your best effort should be your normal.

So when you practice, practice with confidence and a focused and disciplined attitude. Practice not only good physical form and strong technique, but these mental techniques as well. Maintain high levels of concentration and effort during the offseason. Work on developing technique and over-preparing on the fundamentals, to the point that they come as naturally as breathing. It may feel like overkill in the moment, to work on the simple details repeatedly, but fundamentals of your game and sport are solid, they will support you in ways you never imagined.

Have you seen the clip of Ezekiel Elliott of the Dallas Cowboys from the 2018 NFL Season hurdling defender Trey Sullivan from the Philadelphia Eagles? He made a cut at the line of scrimmage to the left, and he's left with a one-on-one match-up with Sullivan, the safety, coming downhill to tackle him. Elliott literally jumped over him, landed on his feet and kept his balance to finish it off for a touchdown. Make it a priority to go to YouTube and find this clip.

First, just watch the clip and enjoy the athleticism.

Next, watch it from the lens of what you've learned so far about confidence.

Third, watch it from the lens of ACE. Does it look any different now watching it the third or fourth time compared to the first?

Elliott was so over-prepared, so thoroughly schooled on the fundamentals, that he could have gone right, left, or through the defender, but in the moment, the other player was obviously going low, so he made an instinctive and creative decision, and his body was able to follow through with it. It doesn't hurt that Elliott was a former track and field star hurdler in high school to his own credit.

ACE can help you do that, not only physically, but mentally—to have the confidence and creativity to respond in the moment to an unexpected situation. Now, I'm not saying you need to be Ezekiel Elliott and jump over people. But imagine the level of preparedness it takes so that a move like that it is a reflex. That's how prepared you need to be.

Elliott's house appears solid. He has the right attitude and confidence to believe he could pull off a play like that before it even began. I don't know if Elliott is an ACE athlete, but he embodies the concepts. Attitude, concentration, and effort. You can see it in a quick snapshot all in that play.

Your past does not dictate your future

It's important not to fall for the mind trap of limiting yourself based on what you've achieved in the past. You may have made mistakes or not lived up to your potential. It doesn't determine what you can do now, let alone what you could do if you applied yourself. You can't change your past, and you don't control your future. That's why the ACE method grounds you where your feet are: in the present moment.

The most crucial ACE component for confidence is Attitude. Attitude is the single biggest predictor of success. To be clear, when I've been referring to a positive attitude in this chapter, I don't mean being positive to the point of disconnecting from reality, pretending everything is great when it's not. No elite athlete stays positive by ignoring the negative. When you lose a game, you feel it. ACE is about putting those negative events in perspective. Once you understand that you can't control them, and they're not your fault, they won't impact your confidence. You're free to do better and work harder in the future, without getting bogged down in negative emotion that has become unproductive.

THE GROUND RULES

1. Be prepared to re-evaluate old habits and assumptions.
2. Don't be afraid to disagree. Critical thinking is an important part of this process.
3. Be determined, patient and consistent; it may take time to see results once you start applying these concepts.
4. Maintain an open, teachable mind.
5. Empty your cup

NINE

GROWTH MINDSET

THE GROUND RULES

1. Be prepared to re-evaluate old habits and assumptions.
2. Don't be afraid to disagree. Critical thinking is an important part of this process.
3. Be determined, patient and consistent; it may take time to see results once you start applying these concepts.
4. Maintain an open, teachable mind.
5. Empty your cup.

It can be challenging when we commit to a new program, like the ACE method, and it doesn't bring miraculous results right away. Often, when we finally do opt to try something new, it's because we really need results, now. But ACE isn't about last-minute miracles. This system is designed to transform your life slowly, over time, and in ways you might not have even thought of yet. Like a house that's just been built and still needs to become a home, a mentally tough athlete still needs some finishing touches. These are character traits that will stand you in good stead for years to come.

Think about a home that's just finished construction and is ready to move in. The walls are up, the flooring is installed, utilities are running.

Imagine the finishing touches you would need to add to that house to make it a home.

List your top 3-5 finishing touches.

Here's my list:

» Furniture (obviously...)
» Pictures on the walls
» A well-stocked pantry and refrigerator

That "new home" smell, whatever it is for you—delicious food, the smell of clean laundry, maybe flowers, or your favorite air freshener.

Like a newly built house, after the solid foundation is set and the walls have made it structurally sound, a mentally tough athlete needs those finishing touches. While important, you can't have them until you've done all the rest of the work.

For a mentally tough athlete, the finishing touches are things like:

» Resiliency,
» Consistency, and
» Patience.

RESILIENCY

Resiliency and consistency are closely related, I should point out. They're like two sides of the same coin. Resiliency is about bouncing back from a negative (or even a positive) event, back to your center line. Consistency is about having a center line to begin with. You can't really have one without the other—they feed into each other. You have to develop them both at the same time.

Have you ever seen a house being built? The work site is a mess. There's no grass, it's just dirt, mud, and the building materials. The project always seems to take longer than it should. You see the work starting in the summer and you figure it'll be done by the fall, but then winter comes, and it's still not done. If you have ever heard people talking about a home they're having built, they are usually complaining about being over budget, or the home not being completed on time.

All of that, too, is a lot like becoming a mentally tough athlete! How many times do we start a season with grand ideas of how disciplined and positive we're going to be? Sometimes we don't hit those goals on time, and sometimes it takes more emotional resources than we thought it would, or we get where we wanted to go in terms of performance, but it doesn't look anything like we thought it would. The truth is, our mental "work site" can be really messy. Our reactions and emotions aren't always neatly compartmentalized, they're often all over the place and getting in the way.

In college, I knew a guy who used to tell me that when he was a kid growing up, one of the ways he made money was on build sites. The workers would give him and his cousins a bucket each and challenge them to pick up as many nails as they could. They got paid a quarter per nail. For a kid, that was pretty good money in the '90s. There were a lot of nails scattered around those work sites.

With ACE, we can run our "work site" a lot more efficiently. It's like having an actual blueprint and schedule instead of just an idea of what the work will look like. ACE gives you the ability to *decide* what you're going to work on, rather than just *hope* that you're feeling positive and disciplined for your next practice.

DEFINITION OF RESILIENCE

Resilience (adj.): Able to withstand or recover quickly from difficult situations or conditions.

IMPORTANCE OF RESILIENCE

Resilience is the weatherproofing on the house. You know it's going to rain eventually, just like you know you're going to lose a game eventually or have a bad practice. What matters is that the house can withstand it; you can still come back the next day and bring your best ACE. In the house of mental toughness, your power and plumbing are set up so that you don't have power outages or clogged toilets, your systems are configured to run smoothly. You can deal with your emotions and process the things that happen so that your athletic performance doesn't break down.

Resilience, much like everything else in this book, isn't something you're just born with. You can, and must, work on it to improve it. Let's say your mental toughness house is a fixer-upper—you know you've got some work to do. Well, get to work! Whatever's wrong with your house, you can improve it. You can find a way to make it better than it was before, even if it's just a tiny improvement every day or every week. Ever watch HGTV, or hear of those people who buy a rundown house say in a suburban city for next to nothing and fix it up by themselves, often turning it into a gorgeous, desired home to live in? If they can do that, you can definitely overhaul your mental framework, piece by piece.

EXAMPLES OF RESILIENCE

Maya is a high school sophomore. She's playing a basketball game, doing a very good job in her position, and all of a sudden her coach pulls her out. Maya doesn't know why. She's been shooting really well, and she has a good free throw percentage. But the coach pulled her, and now she's sitting on the bench wondering if she did something wrong.

Mental resilience looks like Maya saying to herself, *It doesn't matter why I got pulled out. It doesn't matter if I think the coach has the wrong idea about me. I just need to be ready to get back in the game when he calls my number.*

Just a friendly check-in. Although Maya used the resilience mental skill, which principle of ACE did she use?

Non-athletes need resilience, too. College students at the end of the term have to complete two or three mid-terms or finals often times in one day. Let's say a morning exam goes badly, and you're crushed, but you have another one coming up in the afternoon. What do you do? We all know, instinctively, that we can't carry those feelings from the last exam into the next one. You might be feeling fear of failure, guilt over not studying enough, and frustration that the morning exam had questions you didn't think it would, but you have to put all of that aside so you can focus on the next exam.

Then in the evening, or when you're talking to your friends, you work through what happened. "That morning exam was awful, I'm sure I bombed it, I knew as soon as I gave in my paper." That's the right time to work through those emotions—after you're done for the day and you don't need your performance mindset anymore. Resilience isn't about bottling things up or repressing certain feelings. It's about controlling your emotional reaction in the moment and deciding when and where to unpack it.

Quick flashback to Maya again. The time to work through the emotion of being taken out of the game is not while she's sitting on the bench. That's for later when she's at her next practice, or to discuss with the coach personally after the game. Think about it—just because Maya came out of the game for an unknown reason, that coach may want to use Maya to get back in the game in three possessions. But if he looks at the bench and sees her visibly upset, frustrated, and emotional, he may second-guess putting her back in the game at all.

It's not only the big negative events that we require resilience. The small things can be just as important. They can really get under your skin—the offhand remark someone made, someone cutting you off in traffic, a momentary panic because you thought you lost your phone. The small, annoying incidents that leave us flustered and struggling to concentrate—those can really pack a punch in terms of hurting performance.

With ACE, we learn how to handle these uncontrollables. We don't prevent them, but we learn how to bounce back quickly. In a scene from the movie *Rocky Balboa*, his son wants to talk to him outside his restaurant on the sidewalk. He says, "When things got hard, you started looking for something to blame like a big shadow. Let me tell you something you already know. The world ain't all sunshine or rainbows. It's a very mean and nasty place and I don't care how tough you are it will beat you to your knees and keep you there permanently if you let it. You, me, or nobody is gonna hit as hard as life. But it ain't about how hard ya hit, it's about how hard you can get hit and keep moving forward, it's about how much you can take and keep moving forward. That's how winning is done!" He goes on, "Now if you know what you're worth, then go out and get what you're worth! But you gotta be willing to take the hits! And not pointing fingers saying you ain't where you wanna be because of him or her or anybody…cowards do that! And that ain't you!!!"

The reason we can learn and develop our resilience is that stress is a response to an event, like anything else. In the same way that people train for emergency situations by practicing so they don't lose their cool when the real thing happens, you can teach yourself to overcome your stress triggers with ACE.

It's important to remember that stress is unique to the individual. It's not about how big or small something looks on the outside. It's about learning to choose how to react.

For example, something that is a stressor for me is no big deal for my wife, and vice versa. We have a young son, Gabriel. At two years old his table manners need some work. He's starting to be aware that we expect him to behave a certain way at the table, but he's not interested in following Mom or Dad's rules yet. One night, partway through dinner, he got bored and threw his fork on the floor. For me, it was a teaching moment. My wife saw it as a moment to discipline and talk to him. For me, no big deal. For my wife…huge deal.

We see the situation differently, so we respond differently, and we experience different levels of stress accordingly.

I set a timer on my phone for two minutes. I turned to my son, who is laughing and happy now that he'd thrown his fork, and I asked him to pick up the fork and put it on the table. He did it. Then I put the fork back on the floor and asked him to put it on the table again. We practiced this again and again for about two minutes, and about a minute in, he started crying and getting frustrated.

After our two minutes of exercise of picking up his fork I said, "Gabriel, Mommy says to keep the fork on the table. You also need to keep the placemat on the table, OK?" He looked at me and said, "Yes." That's actually a big deal for him because, right now he's struggling with his words and communicating verbally. Fast-forward six months later, he doesn't throw his fork, and when it falls out of his hand or falls off the edge of the table, he looks at my wife and I with his big eyes get and says, "Uhhhhhh – Ohhhhhh," knowing he just made an accident.

During the moment of the fork throwing, my wife took a few big, deep breaths and looked at me. I could tell she was frustrated, and as I can read her mind, I knew she was thinking, *We haven't made any progress on this in a month.* I look to her and say, "Pause for a moment. Smile. Deep breath. Choose a different response. We don't have to be stressed out. It's okay!"

Now, not everyone would think "training my son not to throw things" is a huge victory. First off, those people may not have had the wonderful experience in life to work with a strong-willed two-year-old. Secondly, my wife and I kept our cool, found constructive responses, made a memory that will be shared when he's older, and the best part, no more forks on the floor! Victory. Stress is relative, my friends. We can choose how we respond.

HOW TO BE RESILIENT

Shakespeare wrote in Hamlet, "There is nothing either good or bad, but thinking makes it so."

In other words, we choose our perspective. My two-year-old son throwing things on the floor could have led to an unhappy evening for all of us. It came very close to ruining my wife's dinner as the steam was beginning to pour out her ears. We took at it as a teaching moment to find a way to make it productive and positive.

If you see something as negative and take it personally, and feel like it's out of your control, then you will stress out about it. But by the same token, you can also choose to look for the positive spin, the takeaway for next time, and practice resiliency by teaching yourself how to bounce back from perceived negative events.

Another way of looking at it is this mantra:

Progress, not perfection.

Progress, not perfection means that we should be focusing on the progress we've made, or are making, rather than beating ourselves up for not being perfect. Progress can be incremental.

Jeff is an extraordinary tennis athlete, but he has an emotional problem. When he runs into any kind of adversity, he starts berating himself. He says horrible things to himself. Never to his opponent, only to himself. Jeff gets upset and talks back to his coach, and the situations just build until he's having a meltdown.

I've been working with Jeff for a few months, and we recently sat down to do a review of his progress. I asked him to look back at where he was when we started working together, and he was able to pick out some small victories—some incremental progress.

But the thing is, Jeff has made a lot more progress than he thinks. His coach is receiving praise and great observations on Jeff's play on-court, which definitely wasn't the case a few months ago. Other athletes, parents, and even coaches tell him and Jeff's parents how much he's changed and grown. We see Jeff's progress, but it's hard for him to see it for himself. He still gets discouraged, thinking he hasn't come very far when in fact he has.

It's important to keep an eye out for those little victories, and when they pop up, celebrate them. This doesn't always come naturally; as athletes, we're so good at seeing the progress we have left to make, and we tell ourselves we'll celebrate when we do something big, like winning a championship or getting a scholarship. It's crucial to look for progress, not perfection, and give ourselves a pat on the back when we do make progress. It's not just about making ourselves feel good, it's about reminding ourselves that we *are* making progress, so we don't lose heart and get discouraged.

Just like Jeff, it can be so easy for us to get caught up in negative self-talk and believe that we're not getting anywhere. When we start to lose ground, our motivation slips, we think about quitting, we make a choice to make the sport less of a priority because we believe we're not successful, even though we are.

Emma wants to be a mechanical engineer. She's taking AP classes, and she needs to get really good grades in all of them to get her GPA where it needs to be. A few weeks ago, she told me, "Trevor, I bombed an English test the other day." I asked, "How do you feel about that?"

She said, "Well, I know that I need to do better. I mean, would it keep me from getting into Harvard? Maybe, maybe not. But will it stop me from pursuing mechanical engineering? Not at all. It's not that big of a deal."

Now, she wasn't shrugging off the importance of a bad test. But we had done a lot of work with ACE, about choosing your attitude, and that's what she was demonstrating in that moment. Emma could put that failure in perspective, and be aware that she needed to improve, without taking it personally or stressing out about it or having a meltdown.

Say you're in high school and taking English 11 Literature. Your teacher gives a surprise quiz in class: ten questions. You didn't read the text for that class, so you fail the quiz.

What is your reaction?

Well, no one likes to fail, so I think most people would feel some level of frustration, disappointment, and regret. At the same time, you know, mathematically, that quiz isn't going to affect your overall grade very much. And maybe you make a mental note: *I've gotta make sure I do the readings before class from now on.* Now you're focused on how you can turn this event into a wake-up call for yourself, you're thinking about how you can make sure you do better next time. Put a reminder in your phone to do the readings? Get a friend to study with you?

Whatever the options are, your focus has shifted from this negative incident to how you're going to change your approach for next time. Just like that, instead of feeling bad about the failed quiz, you've got a little energy and motivation going.

RELEVANCE TO ACE

Resilience is about taking control of yourself. You change your attitude by changing what you focus on, and when you choose a different perspective, that allows you to recalibrate the other part of your ACE—your effort and concentration. With a strong ACE foundation, when something goes wrong in your house, you might lose your resilience for a moment, especially if it's a new skill that you're trying to work on. But your ACE foundation will hold up, and you'll be able to come back—it just might be slowly, instead of quickly.

CONSISTENCY

Consistency and confidence are the two main things that parents, athletes, and coaches are constantly asking me about. That's why consistency ended up in the ACE pyramid in the first place.

There are some aspects of a home that we want to be consistent. We want them to always be the same, to always work. Things like opening windows and closing doors—we don't want squeaks, we don't want a door or window that sticks or lets in a draft. You want the plumbing to work—toilets should flush, the faucets and showers should run when you turn them on. There all these little automatic functions in a house that need to be working properly for the home to be comfortable and functional. If those functions aren't working properly, it can damage the other parts of the home, and frustrate the heck out of the occupants.

IMPORTANCE OF CONSISTENCY

As a competitor, you are responsible for bringing a level of consistency day in and day out. This goes for other areas of your life as well—if you have a job, your employer is counting on you to consistently show up on time, and to consistently get your work done. If you have a family, they're counting on you to be consistent when it comes to running errands, paying bills, picking kids up and taking them to their activities. There are a lot of little things that other people depend on you to do, and if you don't, it creates a huge problem very quickly.

If you picture a really strong-willed athlete and name a few traits that you think it takes to be mentally tough, chances are one of those traits will be consistency. When describing a mentally tough athlete, people will typically say, "No matter what, they bring it. Day in, day out."

The funny thing is that if I were to turn the attention on those people, and ask the athletes, "Okay, so how many of you bring it every day?", few put their hands up. We all know we're human and flawed, and it's really hard for us to be consistent in bringing our A-game every day.

But I like to frame this expectation a little differently. The way I see it, it's less about bringing your A-game, and more about showing up. It doesn't matter how you feel in that moment, how loose or how tight your body is feeling; all that matters is showing up, being present, and giving your best ACE that you possibly can, every single day. Because when you practice that deliberately, really cool things will develop.

It's like having friends over and having to get the house ready before they arrive. If you typically keep your house relatively clean, it's not a big deal when people come over. You tidy up a little, and when they walk in, they see it as a clean house, even if it's not completely spotless. But if you are usually a slob and have dishes piled up for a month with flies buzzing around, it's going to take you hours and a lot of effort to clean up. That's the power of consistency—what you do every day builds up, even if you're not going all-out every single day. When something unexpected happens, you're prepared. You have these reserves of strength and discipline you can draw on, that you've been building up the whole time by being consistent.

Concentration is a strong key to consistency; simply by showing up and paying attention, you gain the motivation that will lead you to be consistent. This means showing up on time because you're excited and you want to be there, not because a parent got you out of bed, fed you breakfast and drove you there so you'd be on time.

Like many ACE components, consistency also frees up your mental energy. The more you practice something, the less you have to think about it. If you do certain things at the same time every day, like taking medication or doing a quick mindfulness exercise, it becomes a habit and second nature. When you do it every day, the benefits also stack up.

You know who really understands consistency?

Pets.

If you have a cat or a dog that you feed at the same time every day, they know exactly when that meal is coming. They learn all of your habits—when you get up in the morning, when you go to sleep, when they are going to go for their typical walk or outdoor time(s), what times you generally sit on the couch and watch TV. Pets thrive on routine. They love knowing what's going to happen and when.

I recently heard a tip for remembering to take medication. If you give your cat a treat every day right before you take your pill, you might forget your pill one day, but your cat definitely won't. They'll come bug you until you remember. For animals, consistency is absolutely crucial. It's how they know everything is okay in their world. Consistency is really important for us humans too, and we thrive on it as well.

HOW TO BE CONSISTENT

COMMIT TO CHANGE

The first step to develop consistency is to commit to change. It's really easy to say you want to be a better athlete, who doesn't want that? But what matters is the little choices you make.

For example, let's say you want to be a college basketball player. Let's say you know that there's an early timeslot at the gym, 7AM on Saturday mornings, where you have permission to go to the gym and shoot until 8AM. After that, the gym is being used for other activities and you won't have access for the rest of the day till late that night.

That early morning timeslot is your best opportunity to get extra shots in, in a great environment. But if you're out late on Friday night, do you really have the commitment to get out of bed early the next morning and give great attitude, great concentration, and great effort towards that early morning workout?

Commitment to change is the foundation for consistency. If you want it bad enough, you will get out of bed. You will show up on time. You will find those extra opportunities and be there for them, every time. You'll be consistent, not because you're trying to, but as a side effect of wanting to be a good athlete and do whatever it takes.

MICRO-REWARDS

When you set a goal and achieve it, take a break and enjoy yourself: a micro-reward. If you have a tendency towards being a workaholic, or if you have some anxiety and it pushes you to work yourself to exhaustion, micro-rewards are very effective for giving you a stopping point so that you don't burn yourself out.

What I recommend is to set a goal for an amount of training, or a time period, that is productive and will help you. Practice for a few hours, achieve your goal, and then take the afternoon off—go for a hike, go fishing, hang out with friends. Then plug back in and set new goals and start the cycle again.

RELEVANCE TO ACE

Change is inevitable; growth is 100% optional.

It's not just a commitment to change that you need, it's a commitment to growth. To develop consistency, you need to be able to choose what you're going to concentrate on, every time, and you gain that ability by practicing it. It's the same with effort—you need to consistently bring your best effort. If you can't bring the ACE components consistently, your game will really suffer. In fact, consistency is key for a lot of success in life. If you do an amazing thing once, it goes on Youtube and gets some views for a while before being forgotten. But if you can make a career out of doing something consistently, you'll find success.

PATIENCE

It takes time to finish a house. Rome wasn't built in a day and neither is a mentally tough athlete. It takes patience because you're not going to start off with all of these mental tools fully developed and ready to go. You have to build them and implement them in your routine, and it will take time to get there. To really see the benefit of the ACE method, you have to be willing to be disciplined and patient over a long period of time.

You often hear coaches say, "trust the process." To be as successful as possible with ACE, you must practice it consistently.

EXAMPLES OF PATIENCE

If you want instant food, you can make it in a microwave, but how satisfying will it really be? If you want to make amazing food, you're going to use something that takes a little time: a barbecue, a slow cooker, a smoker, shoot bake something in the oven!

So if you want to be a mentally tough athlete, what tools are you using? This sounds like a simple question, but many athletes think that athletic achievement is something you're born to do, or you're not. This question reframes it as a question of commitment, dedication, and work. What *tools* are you using to make yourself a better athlete? Because you're not born with all the athletic talent you'll ever have.

Athletic success is about the skills we develop, not about the traits we were born with. Yes, if you're 6'10", that height might help you become a gifted basketball player. But then again, it might not! You might still be clumsy or slow. The physical trait of height is there, but it needs to be accompanied by skills and a work ethic.

I remember going to a basketball camp at a college in my home state of Iowa when I was in 8th grade going into 9th. That summer camp showed me something interesting. I met these two guys from a Wisconsin high school, both 11th graders with one being 6'9" and the other being 6'10". They had the physical trait of height, but they couldn't catch a quick dump pass when I was driving through the lane to save their life. Not to mention their inability to dunk. Yes, you heard that right. Tall dudes who couldn't catch the ball and dunk. Great guys, lazy work ethic, but they accepted their height as a natural advantage that didn't need any more work.

HOW TO BE PATIENT

Imagine you're in one of my workshops, standing in a group of your peers.

I start by asking, "How good do you want to be as an athlete?"

I ask one of the athletes, and they say, "Good."

I say, "How good is good?"

They say something like, "Well, I want to be pretty good."

I say, "Well, what does that mean?"

Finally, they respond with a little fire, "I really want to be good."

I say to the room, "You know, it took me asking three times for this athlete to convince me that he wants to be really good. If you really wanted it, I should have been able to feel it in your eyes, your voice and your body language the first time."

Then I pick another athlete and ask them, "How good do you want to be?"

Of course, by now they know exactly what to do. They say with some energy, "I want to be great!"

I say, "OK, that's awesome, I feel the energy." And then I take out a roll of duct tape and put a line on the floor.

I stand on one side of the tape and say, "On this side of the tape, you want to be the best player that you can be." Then I step over to the other side and say, "On this side of the tape, you would like to be great. You would like to be good. You would like to improve."

I address the group: "You know where most athletes your age live? They spend a lot of time doing this." And I walk in circles over the line and back, again and again.

As I'm walking over the "great" side of the line, I say, "You know what's happening over here? I just had a great victory, I got promoted to team captain, I just had an awesome test score, I'm super motivated to be great."

Then I walk to the other side of the line. "Over here, I just lost that tough match, I messed up on a test, my friends are mad at me."

Then I ask, "Based on what I just did, what side of the tape do you think I'm on?"

I typically don't get a straight answer. The athletes might try to explain why one side might have more of a weight than the other, but I point out that as I'm walking back and forth across the line, I'm saying the right things about wanting to be great, but clearly my actions are saying otherwise. My motivation and drive keep shifting based on the events that are happening.

Do you think that's a problem? Shouldn't you know where an athlete stands in terms of his/her motivation?

It's definitely a problem.

You know what the solution is? Make a choice. Are you in or are you out? It's like hitting a light switch—it's either on or off. You're either 100% in, and *on*, or you're less than 100%, that is to say, *off*. Like many things about the ACE method, it simplifies your life. You make the decision one time, and then after that, you always know the choice to make. If you decide you're all in, then any time you have a choice to make—showing up to an early, optional practice, putting in some extra work in the evenings, doing some research—you don't have to think about it. You already know what choice you've made. From then on, these other qualities that we've discussed: resilience, consistency, and patience—will all be easier to practice.

I want to close this chapter with a reminder that the ACE method requires 100% commitment because you have to apply it to 100% of your game and your life. You can't pick and choose which areas to apply it to. You can't decide to ignore the Attitude part of ACE and apply the rest. It doesn't work like that. ACE requires you to be constantly asking, "Am I practicing great ACE right now? Am I still all in?"

If you have a crack in your foundation, water will get in and start to erode that foundation. Over time, it will make the house unstable and you won't be able to live in it until you've fixed the foundation.

Someday, if you're looking for a house to buy, and you find two that you really like, but then learn that one of them has a cracked foundation that has to be repaired, how likely are you to buy that damaged house in *that* condition? In the same way, when a coach is considering recruiting two athletes with similar talent and grades, but one of them has a wonderful positive and resilient attitude and the other is selfish and toxic, who do you think the coach will recruit and select first?

So as an athlete regardless of your age, my advice is to work on your foundation immediately. Because if you have cracks or chips in your foundation now, it becomes exponentially tougher to develop farther no matter what else you try to improve upon. That's what ACE is for: creating that solid foundation that you can build on. As you grow and progress, you'll need to *maintain* that foundation. There are always things that can come along and damage it if you're not careful, for example, tree roots or water damage. The traits we looked at in this chapter, resiliency, consistency, and patience, are also part of that maintenance and self-awareness that you need to have.

Here's an old-school quote that sums this up really well:

A man's mind may be likened to a garden which may be intelligently cultivated or allowed to run wild. But whether cultivated or neglected, it must and will bring forth. If no useful seeds are put into it, then an abundance of useless weed seeds will fall therein and will continue to produce their kind.
—James Allen, *As a Man Thinketh*

It's saying that a person's mind is like a garden. You can tend to it or you can forget about it, but either way, it's going to grow something. If you don't tend to it and grow useful things, like herbs, fruits, and vegetables, then it will go wild and grow weeds.

Our minds are the same. We can pay attention to what we allow ourselves to consume as we learned in the first few chapters, or we can just forget about it and do whatever we feel like. Either way, our minds are going to produce thoughts, behaviors, and actions.

"As a man thinketh in his heart, so is he." (Proverbs 23:7)

THE GROUND RULES

1. Be prepared to re-evaluate old habits and assumptions.
2. Don't be afraid to disagree. Critical thinking is an important part of this process.
3. Be determined, patient and consistent; it may take time to see results once you start applying these concepts.
4. Maintain an open, teachable mind.
5. Empty your cup.

TEN

STRAIGHT TALK: LET'S USE ACE

THE GROUND RULES

1. Be prepared to re-evaluate old habits and assumptions.
2. Don't be afraid to disagree. Critical thinking is an important part of this process.
3. Be determined, patient and consistent; it may take time to see results once you start applying these concepts.
4. Maintain an open, teachable mind.
5. Empty your cup.

I'm going to describe some techniques you may not have taken seriously before, I hope you'll set aside your assumptions and just try the exercises. You might be surprised by how much they can help. This chapter also describes long-term practices that will yield better and better results the longer you use them. These methods will help you over the length of your career, and hopefully for your entire life, but they may not be at full strength in 24 hours when you go to use them for the first time.

DEEP BREATHING—THE MAGIC ELIXIR

Deep breathing works. It works. Period. End stop.

Meet Mike, pictured below deep breathing in Badwarer Basin, California (Death Valley)—

Mike's one of a kind. A man's man.

And one that comes with many titles—some too crazy to make up. Let's start with some easy ones. A father, a grandpa, dog lover, a nature enthusiast. Former Marine. Prolific car camper—even though he can afford any hotel. Former Marine of the year, former D1 athlete (soccer & track). Trained Special Forces soldiers for nearly a decade—sport & performance psych related work. Sales leader. Entrepreneur. Social media poster—find him here @SportsPsyMike (Twitter) and College professor, college football coach (even though he never played), and one diaphragmatic-belly-breathing, loving, wealth-of-knowledge-teaching friend.

My good friend, Mike Hatfield, refers to deep breathing as the "magic elixir" because it's so powerfully calming. Deep breathing means breathing from your belly—with each breath in, your diaphragm (or belly) expands, and with each breath out, it pulls in or contracts again. If you've ever sung in a choir or taken elocution lessons, this is similar to the breathing that they recommend for singing or giving a speech.

To get the best results, you should be practicing deep breathing frequently and in lots of different settings. If you just learn deep breathing 24 hours before a big game and try it the day of, it might not be very useful to you right away. The more you practice deep breathing, the more your body gets used to responding and relaxing. It learns what to do. So breathing is one of those skills that's great in an emergency, but you should really be practicing it on a regular basis. It's also very accessible—you can practice taking a deep breath in certain situations, or a daily meditation, or during any one of many mindfulness apps and exercises out there.

Breathing really ties into the ACE components because you need to have:

» the belief that it can help you,
» the presence of mind and effort to do the deep breathing exercises,
» concentration to focus yourself on the breathing and the present moment.

Not for nothing, breathing is also something that is in your circle of control. You can put your confidence and concentration in your breathing and direct your energy and effort there. It's not a distraction or an uncontrollable.

IMPORTANCE OF VAGUS NERVE

There is a long nerve in your body, called the Vagus nerve or more commonly known as "the Wandering nerve," and it begins from your medulla oblongata (think Adam Sandler's movie, The Waterboy) brainstem all the way down to your belly, through your diaphragm.

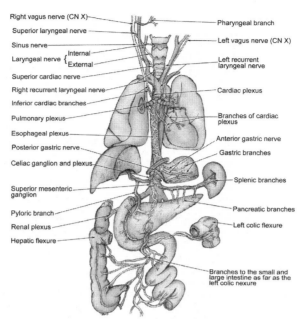

Vagus Nerve Anatomy, Ted L Tewfik, Medscape
https://emedicine.medscape.com/article/1875813-overview

It touches different organs in your midsection along its path such as your pancreas, gallbladder, liver, intestines, kidneys, heart, and lungs. The Vagus nerve has control over a wide range of many bodily functions. Most of us have never heard of it, but it's well-known in the medical community.

Here's where this Vagus nerve stuff gets cool. When you practice deep breathing with your diaphragm, it forces you to use your lungs at greater capacity, which means a few awesome things.

1. You receive more oxygen rich blood into your bloodstream and directly to your brain

2. The diaphragm, which you cannot control or move around like you can your arms and legs, is a muscle that expands when you breathe with your belly. When expanding (while belly breathing – on purpose), it essentially massages the Vagus nerve and activates the relaxation response throughout the body

3. When you breathe, it immediately can help release physical tension or emotional stress

If you think of any contemplative activity, like yoga or meditation, deep breathing is always at the core of that activity. You can just do the deep breathing associated with those activities on its own to get a lot of the same benefits quickly.

Deep breathing also has the emotional benefit of getting you out of your head and bringing your focus to your physical body. When we focus on our body, we're focusing on something concrete and tangible, unlike most of the abstract thoughts, distractions, and noise in our head. It makes it easier to let go of the things that are bothering us.

ACTIVATES RELAXATION RESPONSE

The practice and application of deep breathing shows up in just about any performance realm you can imagine. From sports to school (yes, test anxiety is real my friends…), to the military, martial arts, meditation disciplines, powerlifting, and even in the medical communities! For the record, this is *far* from an exhaustive list.

In the military, they train snipers how to lower your heart rate and shoot in-between heartbeats on the exhale of breath. In sports, there's a good chance you may naturally take a breath before a free throw or a serve, or even if you get benched and come out of the game.

Some sports, like swimming, treat breathing like an athletic skill that is no different than their freestyle or backstroke.

During anything uncontrollable that may be happening, you can usually control your response a little better if you're watching your breathing. Many of us instinctively take a deep breath before doing something big.

IMMEDIATELY FELT IN ANY STRESSFUL SITUATION

Earlier in this book, I made a mention of responding to situations based on emotions. Now that we know a little more about ACE and how breathing can help us, consider the following again.

When was the last time you made a really good decision when you were emotionally charged, or in a high-stress state? Most athletes think on this for a bit and come back with a blank stare of acknowledgment that they can't come up with an example off the top of their head. Can we make really good and sound decisions when we're emotionally charged? I'm not saying you can't, but I do know that when we're emotionally reacting to situations, there's a very good chance that we're not doing a good job of thinking logically at that exact moment.

When you're in a stressful situation, you need a way to regain your composure and think critically about how you want to respond. Deep breathing can deliver that composure instantly. The more you practice it, the more you condition yourself to respond to this technique, the more you'll be able to avoid "mental mistakes" in the stressful moments in the middle of a game. You'll have the skill to take a breath and consider your options to respond, rather than reacting impulsively or emotionally. Deep breathing doesn't guarantee that you will make the perfect choice every time—there are still so many other uncontrollable variables—but you'll be in a much better position to think, respond, and find success.

Deep breathing will become a part of your essential toolkit, something you do almost automatically, just as ACE will.

3X3X3 BREATHING

If you get pre-game jitters or stage fright, all you have to do is find a quiet place and practice a deep breathing exercise. Put one hand on your tummy and eliminate all movement from your shoulders and chest. You should feel your hand moving while you're doing this activity. I like to go by threes: breathe in for three seconds through your nose, hold it for three seconds, breathe out through your mouth for three seconds. Depending on what article, research, or philosophy you follow, you'll read different rhythm counts and different experts telling you what's most effective. I've tried many, and trained many, but the most effective one that works for me is 3x3x3.

If you are an athlete playing a quick response sport, try shortening it to two seconds, or utilize a pause in the action to get in a quick 3x3x3 cycle. The important thing is, you're being conscious of your breathing and you're focusing on breathing through your belly/ diaphragm.

Ultimately, what matters in sports is being able to adapt. A breathing practice that works for you is better than nothing. If you only have time for a single deep breath, then do that. It will still help.

You must develop this skill off the field, much like I did for my wedding day. If I had never practiced it before would it have worked as well? Probably not. Could I have calmed down in the moment using it for the first time? Absolutely, but it may have taken much longer and I may have had different moments of anxiety creep up the rest of the day between ceremony and end of the reception.

REFOCUS ROUTINE ON ACE

As a mental conditioning coach, one of the most important things I teach is a refocus routine. It's for the times when an uncontrollable happen—maybe you trip and fall and the other team scores, or you're a pitcher and you give up a monster hit to the other team's batter. After each play, after each pitch, we need to reset.

When bad things happen, our job is to find ways to quickly re-center ourselves so we can be fresh and focused for the next play. This is not to say that you never reflect on what happened. There will be time for that, reflecting on the game is an important way to improve. But during the game is not the time for that. In the game, frustrating uncontrollables can happen, and if you let them, it has the potential to derail your performance. Your objective is to manage your emotions and energy to try to keep them as steady and constant as possible.

If I were to walk up in the middle of one of your games, I shouldn't be able to tell from your body language whether you're winning or losing. Your stance, your expression, the way you move, it should all look as similar as possible regardless of what's happening in the game. The refocus routine isn't about bottling up your emotions and not dealing with things. It's about setting aside the things that can wait while you attend to what matters right now.

Nearly every single sport has a break in action, whether it's a lot or a little, providing you an opportunity to reset. Even in professional darts, you take turns throwing, so you get a quick moment after your turn. In competitive rifle shooting, there are breaks between the rounds. I can't believe I'm referencing it, but in ESPN's professional Cornhole circuit, each player has alternating shots, and walking to the other end to pick up the bags gives the players a quick pause and break. Basketball, volleyball, soccer, tennis, all have breaks in action. Even during gameplay, if the ball is out of your area or goes out of bounds, you may have several extended seconds here and there where you're not doing anything.

Mike Hatfield and I ran the numbers one time, and there is a surprising amount of time in each sport, during the game, where an individual athlete is just standing around. Not for long periods at a stretch, but there's generally a minute here, a minute there, where you're waiting for something to happen, or getting ready for the next play, or just watching because the ball hasn't come to you yet.

That's not dead time. It's not time for you to stand around and decide where you want to eat after the game. That's time for your reset routine.

THE REFOCUS ROUTINE: WHAT NOT TO DO

When I was a Junior in college playing baseball, my mother came down with a mysterious back problem. She was in crippling, mind-numbing pain and no one could figure out why. They eventually determined it was some sort of viral infection that was attacking the nervous system in her back through one of her lumbar vertebrae. For several days they were just running tests and coming up with nothing: MRIs, CAT scans, ultrasounds, bloodwork. I watched her arms being poked like pincushions and veins collapsing due to dehydration. Painful.

I took a leave of absence from baseball for a few days because as a family we were so worried about my mom. We didn't know if her illness was terminal, or degenerative, if there was a cure, if she'd be fine after a few days or never recover and be bed-ridden the rest of her life. Truly we didn't know. To this day, we don't know exactly how she caught the virus. The infectious disease specialist said it could have come from something as small as a hangnail.

But after a couple of days, we realized there was nothing I could do for her in the hospital. Mom didn't want me missing time from the season, and as a matter of fact, she was mad that I missed a game to be with her in the hospital. As difficult as it was, I honored her wishes and went back.

This was before I had learned ACE or really knew much at all about mental toughness. My first game back I don't recall playing well. I was there in body but not in spirit. I remember I couldn't even stand still—I kept stepping from side to side, back and forth and was very on edge, full of jitters. The second we got out of the post-game brief, I was on my phone calling my family to get an update on my mom.

That's an example of what can happen when you get hit with a terrible uncontrollable and you don't have ACE or any practices to fall back on to support your mental focus. No foundation, nothing to stand on. I just fell apart. I wanted to be with my mom, *and* I wanted to be playing my sport because my team needed me, and I needed them! I was torn and truthfully, I couldn't focus on either.

Hindsight is amazing. We can typically see how to do things very differently if we were to be given a second chance. Here's what I would do differently, knowing what I know now.

First things first: **Attitude**. I would ask myself, can I be present and committed at this game right now, or not? If not, I'm going to take myself out because my team deserves better than me being split-minded. Notice, I never said I'm going to feel happy and have a positive attitude. I'm scared for my mom right now—it's not realistic to expect myself to be positive right now. What I *can* do is be present and committed.

Next, **Concentration**. I decided to stay in the game, so now I need to make sure I can focus. I'm shutting my phone off or giving it to a coach who can monitor and tell me if there's an update, so I don't have to think about it. I'm trusting them to notify me if something is urgent. Focus on playing the game and living pitch to pitch. Inning to inning.

Finally, **Effort**. I'm mentally preparing myself to give 100% in this game. No half-in, half-out—no lost moments or opportunities because I was staring off into space thinking about my problems. My energy and effort is 100% on this field for the next three hours. For the length of this game, I'm bringing all of my energy to this sport. When the game is over and it is time to think about everything else that's going on, I'll still have time and energy for that, and I'll deal with it then. But not now.

Would my attention in the game have been different had I used ACE? No doubt. I didn't ask if my results would have been different. I asked if my *attention* would be.

It's like if you have two tests to study for, algebra and chemistry, and you have two hours in the library to study. It would be easy to feel overwhelmed about everything you have to do, to spin your wheels and not accomplish much. But instead, the smart approach is to set a 60-minute timer and say to yourself, *For the next 60 minutes, I'm all about algebra. Nothing else exists.* If 60 minutes is too long, then take it 10 or 15 minutes at a time, and whenever your concentration starts to waver, go through your refocus routine. Maybe it's a word that you write at the top of your notes to keep you motivated. Maybe you go refill your water bottle at the water fountain and do some deep breathing—whatever works for you. The point is, you limit your focus to just one thing for a specific period of time. Maybe you also create a to-do list with the other things that you need to remember to do so you won't forget them. That will help your mind relax and re-focus on the task at hand.

IT'S NOT A RITUAL

Because I'm talking about routines, I want to take a minute to clarify something. This is a routine, it's not a ritual. Rituals to me are associated with superstition, like athletes who have lucky socks that they wear for every game, or athletes who always play with certain gear, like compression leggings, to the point that if they don't have that particular item, it will throw their game off. Now, consistency is key for athletes, as we discussed in previous chapters, and a lot of time athletes create that sense of structure with their rituals. The problem comes in when you allow the ritual to control you and how you let it impact you when it's off.

If you're a golfer and you like to get onto the putting green an hour before your tee off to stretch, go over all your gear, and warm up, what if something uncontrollable happens? What if there's some bad weather coming in, so they move up your time? Now you only have half an hour for your routine instead of an hour, or maybe you are only allowed ten minutes, or no time at all? Is that going to throw you off your game? Is it going to cost you strokes on the course? Because if so, that ritual is not serving you. It's holding you back.

PICK A, C, OR E TO DIAL INTO 100%

When you're using your refocus routine, if there's an element of your game that's just a little bit off, I encourage you to pick just one of the three ACE components and dial into it 100%. Focus your whole routine specifically on one of those areas and see the difference.

Sofia, the tennis player, knows she needs to stay positive. So during her refocus routine, she's going to focus 100% on her attitude.

When she does the first step, the release, she's reminding herself: *Let's let that last point go. It's no big deal. Who cares?*

For the second step, the planning phase, she's choosing the positive attitude that's going to go with her strategy in the next round.

Finally, for the refocus step, Sofia has the choice of the smile or the deep breath. In this case, she goes for the smile.

Instead of trying to attend to all three components, she just picked attitude, and customized her routine so that each step supports a better attitude. As an athlete, you will typically know what element of your game is off, but if you're feeling unsure, I encourage you to check in with a parent or coach.

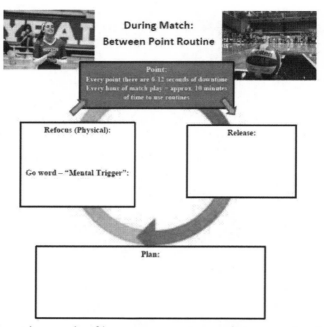

A quick example of how a reset routine can be generated and used for any sport and any athlete

MULTI-TASK DEBUNKED

Is it possible to multi-task? Take a minute and write down what you think. Yes or no?

If you wrote yes, write down some reasons why you said yes.

I'm guessing your reasons would be something like, *I can walk and chew gum, I can talk to a passenger in the front seat of the car while we drive.*

Well, experienced drivers can drive and talk to a passenger in the front seat. But when you're a new driver, they advise you not to even turn on the radio because you need to pay such careful attention to what you're doing and avoid significant distractions. In Iowa at age 14 you can get your learners permit, and if you live far enough away from school, you can apply and obtain a school permit where it allows you to drive to and from school (without a license) and without a licensed driver supervising you. Allow me to share, when I was a new driver, my parents wouldn't let me drive with a passenger while using my school permit, #1 because in Iowa it's the law, and #2 because they knew it's a distraction.

Productivity experts say that even when we think we're multitasking, most of the time we are actually just shifting our attention from one thing to another really quickly. In an example like walking and chewing gum, you're probably not focusing on either of those things because you've been doing them for years and they've become automatic.

Walking, chewing gum, texting on your phone and crossing a busy intersection, though, is a different story. Assuming you want to survive and not get hit by oncoming traffic, you'll look up from your texting to check the traffic lights and see if any cars are coming. If there's traffic and you can't walk right away, you'll look back down at your phone. You would describe what you're doing as multitasking, because you're walking, chewing gum, texting, *and* crossing a road, but actually your attention is just shifting from one thing to another really quickly—first the traffic lights, then back to your phone, then probably back to the traffic in a second or two to see if you can go yet, then back to your phone.

Besides that, we also know that it takes a certain amount of time working at a task before you start to enter a flow state. For most people, that time is about 15-20 minutes. It takes you that long to settle into a task you've just started, to become focused and productive. So if you're doing homework, listening to music and messaging your friends, your productivity slips a little every time your attention shifts from one thing to another, because you're starting a new task every few minutes. Instead of entering a flow state, which is the most focused and productive (and enjoyable) way to work, you'll keep working on a superficial level, not really engaging with any of the tasks.

3 SCENARIOS

Scenario 1: Coach pulls you out of the game because you've made mistakes.

Let's say you're using ACE as your go-word. You can start with **A** and dial into your Attitude 100%. You might say to yourself:

It doesn't matter that coach pulled me out. I'm out because I made mistakes. So now I'm going to watch my position and study my opponent to find ways to beat them if and when I get another chance. This is an opportunity for me to learn and refocus for my next moment.

Scenario 2: Your parent(s) and coach are upset that you're not making it to practices on time and are showing up late to school on a regular basis.

Assuming your go-word is ACE, this time let's look at **E** for Effort and dial into that 100%.

The first thing you'll see is that your effort and values must change immediately. You must re-evaluate why you go to school and why playing your sport is important to you. Your coach and parents must not want success more than you do. If that happens continuously, you must be willing to look deep within yourself and challenge your previous assertions on what you value and prioritize. You need to focus on increasing the effort you're putting out immediately.

Isaac was late to school almost every day. He was late for every morning workout. He was close to getting suspended for being tardy, and he was the quarterback of the football team! So, I reached out to him and asked what was going on. His response was, "My alarm goes off...but I don't get out of bed."

I asked him several other questions. Each question I asked, I heard a different answer. It dawned on me what the issue was and I wasn't going to hold back.

"You know what it sounds like? My friend, it's not a motivational problem. It's a lack of values." Silence on the other end of the line.

I continued, "Did you know that a kid with a high school degree earns about $2.5 million less in a lifetime than a kid with a college education, and if you go on to an advanced degree it's worth another $1.9 million?" Full transparency... I didn't actually know these numbers off the top of my head. I made them up to motivate him. But the basic principle I was getting at holds true—education does translate to higher wages over most people's lifetime.

I went on, "If you want to keep this up, you can, but just so you know, there's a consequence for everything you choose to do or not do. Right now, you are earning these consequences", meaning the suspension.

We talked it over a bit more, and I said, "You know what it comes down to? It comes down to values and effort. That alarm clock goes off in the morning, you have to have the response of, *Damnit, I've got to get up and get going.* Even though your bed is comfortable, you're sleepy and still sore from the day before, you have to get up and give a 100% effort with whatever energy you've got on that day.

Effort doesn't stand alone, it often comes out of your attitude and your values. If you see something as important, you'll put the effort in. If not, you won't. So if you're struggling to find the effort for something you need to do, often there's an attitude or value adjustment that needs to happen, and that's the first place your effort needs to go—towards your attitude.

Sometimes you will have to lead with your strength. I do recommend starting with fixing your attitude if you can because then your effort will naturally flow from there, but if you are finding it really difficult to adjust your attitude, go with effort. You'll show up to the early morning practice, you'll be all grumpy and still rubbing the sleep out of your eyes, you might be mad at the coach—but you should still get credit. You showed up.

Your effort is there, now you just need your attitude to catch up. If you keep it up, eventually your attitude will follow. So if you want to lead with your effort because you're better at forcing yourself to do something than changing your attitude, I'll take it. It's a start. Over time you'll get used to it and realize, *Hey, this would be a lot more enjoyable if my attitude were better.*

> **Scenario 3:** An athlete is playing a game and can hear parents criticizing the coach's decisions, as well as other members of the crowd yelling at specific players and the team.

Your go-word is ACE. This time, we'll dial into **C**oncentration 100%. Remind yourself that you can't control anyone else—all you can control is what you're choosing to concentrate and focus on. So refocus back on the task at hand, whatever it is—complete the pass, dribble the ball, focus on the play. Let all those other distractions melt away and drift on by.

Negative thoughts in our heads are like mosquitoes hitting your windshield. You've got two choices: clean them off or let them build up until you can't see any more. In this analogy, cleaning the mosquitoes off means just letting go of those negative thoughts. They're not real, and they're not important. Just wipe them away.

It sounds easy, but I know it's not. Clearing negative thoughts from your mind is something you get better at with practice—it's a skill you can develop. Make an "IF/THEN" statement: *If people start shouting and heckling, and it's getting to me, I'm going to use my refocus routine to get my head back in the game.* If you don't have a refocus routine set up, I highly recommend creating one and practicing it. It will be your standby in so many different situations.

THE GROUND RULES

1. Be prepared to re-evaluate old habits and assumptions.
2. Don't be afraid to disagree. Critical thinking is an important part of this process.
3. Be determined, patient and consistent; it may take time to see results once you start applying these concepts.
4. Maintain an open, teachable mind.
5. Empty your cup.

ELEVEN

EXTENDING ACE BEYOND SPORTS

THE GROUND RULES

1. Be prepared to re-evaluate old habits and assumptions.
2. Don't be afraid to disagree. Critical thinking is an important part of this process.
3. Be determined, patient and consistent; it may take time to see results once you start applying these concepts.
4. Maintain an open, teachable mind.
5. Empty your cup.

Worry and anxiety are often longstanding habits in our lives; we assume that our worry is an appropriate response to the situation. I'm going to discuss ways to get away from that thinking, and to remember that worrying actually doesn't change anything, for you or for anyone else that you're trying to help. To really absorb this message, you have to let go of the assumption that your anxiety is useful. When it comes to performance, it isn't.

ACE isn't just for sports. Sports is like a high-octane example of how you can apply ACE, but these concepts can actually be used to deal with everyday issues and challenges too. Any obstacle you run into traces its roots back to at least one ACE component, if not all three. The only circle of control is you.

Performance anxiety isn't just for athletes. Whether it's social situations, or acting and performing, or you just hate taking tests, or going for job interviews…everyone gets some level performance anxiety. You'll often hear people talk about this anxiety like it's something they were born with, "I just always get nervous when I have to speak in front of people."

But anxiety is often the result of habits that we formed long ago—so long ago that we don't even think about them anymore. They just seem to come naturally. We develop habits, and then our habits develop us. That's the power of habits, they can be used to either build us up or tear us down.

If you start to think about the things that make you nervous, you'll probably start to notice a longstanding pattern. You might even remember an incident early on in your life when the anxiety seemed to start. In other words, anxiety might come naturally to you now, but it didn't always. That means you can change it.

Whoever you are today, you can become someone different tomorrow. You can develop new habits, a new perspective, a new way of expressing who you are.

In an earlier chapter, we talked about how the mind needs to be where your feet are, in the present moment. When you focus too much on the past or the future, you tend to encounter anxiety. When you're focusing too much on the past, you might be remembering past incidents where things didn't go well—over and over again. You might be overthinking something a friend said to you. When you're focusing too much on the future, that could mean fixating on worst-case scenarios instead of being optimistic or hopeful. It means experiencing anxiety over situations that may well never eventuate. Either way, your mind is in the wrong time zone—you're not focused on the here and now. That disconnect creates nervous energy that becomes anxiety. The solution is to bring your concentration back to the present moment.

CONNECT BACK TO ACE

Here's how to do that.

When you find yourself fixating on the past or present, I encourage you as a reader to shift your concentration back to the moment and focus on the W.I.N. principle—What's Important Now.

Let's say I'm a basketball player. I've just been fouled and I have seventeen seconds left to make two free throws. I'm standing on the court ready to make my free throws, and I'm starting to panic. Why?

Because I've been missing free throws. My practices haven't been great. And in this moment, the game could come down to me making these free throws. Around me, the gym is rocking and roaring. So, I'm feeling very anxious right about now. Heart racing. Palms sweating. What do I do?

The W.I.N. principle is about filtering out the noise in those pressure-filled moments. I ask myself, *what's important right now?* I start eliminating things that aren't important. By the way. Take a deep belly breath or two.

The Bible says:

...do not be worried about your life as to what you'll eat, what you drink, not for your body as what you put on. Is life more important than food, body more than clothing, look at the birds of the air that they do not sow, nor reap, nor gather in barns, yet your heavenly father feeds them. Are you not worth more than they? And **who of you, by being worried, can add a single hour to your life.** *"*

(Matthew 6:25)

Finally, this verse sums it all up:

So, do not worry about tomorrow, for tomorrow will take care of itself. Each day has enough trouble of its own.

(Matthew 6:34)

Take this as a direct commandment...we are *not* meant to worry and be anxious!

Let's take that emphasis on what is worth worrying about and what isn't, and apply it to our free throw example.

Is it important, right now, that the crowd is going nuts? No, because I don't control it.

Is it important that I've missed shots like this before? No, because I can't change and control my previous outcomes.

So what *is* important?

What's important is, I know exactly how to shoot and make a free throw. I've practiced it. Thousands of times. I can do it in my sleep, and I can do it right now. I'm going to take two deep breaths, focus on and trust my routine, and follow through with my hand. That's what I can control.

That's how you ground yourself in those moments of anxiety— you filter everything else out and go back to your training.

I want to point out a trap that a lot of people can fall into in these moments, whether you're a coach or an athlete.

It's easy to say to yourself, or for a coach to say to you, "Okay, you've got this. Now, *go sink those shots.*" You don't control whether or not you sink the shot. You only control your technique. As we know through ACE, it's not helpful to focus on something you don't control.

What would work better is to say to yourself, *Okay. Focus on your routine, take a deep breath, and follow through.* That's your technique—you can control whether or not you execute it. That's where your focus should belong. You see, even though the moment seems really pressure-filled, loud and overwhelming, you don't need to do anything amazing in order to perform. Fundamentals pay off here. Focusing on the here and now pays off.

The W.I.N. principle is just another way of using ACE to ground yourself and bring your concentration back to the present moment.

Let's take a non-sports example.

Let's say you're trying out for a part in a play, and you're really anxious because you really want the part. First of all, remember that it's not a bad thing to feel anxious because you want something so badly. That shows you care and you're passionate. So it may feel uncomfortable at times, but it's actually a good thing.

Secondly, it's normal to be at least a little nervous. Remember the expression, "butterflies in your stomach" to describe the feeling in your belly when you get nervous? I use that expression because sometimes you really do feel a sort of fluttery sensation in your belly when you're nervous.

Now imagine a butterfly cage with ten butterflies in it. Imagine that you can watch them fly around, and study each one because there's just ten in the cage. It's beautiful.

Now add 5,000 butterflies to that cage. Still beautiful? No! Now it's chaos. Those butterflies would be bumping into each other, hurting their wings, not able to come to rest.

So, it's okay to have a few "butterflies" before a performance, as long as you're not getting overwhelmed. It's not okay to have so many butterflies that it's chaotic.

If you're feeling like there are 5,000 butterflies in your stomach, then you need to do something to get those butterflies under control. First, if you're feeling really nervous, you can start with some deep breathing to help you calm down again. Once you're in the process of bringing a sense of calm, answer the W.I.N. principle to bring the butterfly count down a few notches.

Just as we did in the previous example, we're going to filter out the parts of the situation that aren't important.

Is it important to focus on whether or not you get the role in the play? No, because you don't control that.

Is it important to focus on whether or not the judges think you did a good job? No, because you don't control the judges.

What *is* important?

What's important is that you practiced for this moment, so now all you can do is go out there and give it your best. Whatever happens, happens.

Notice with every single example we are drawing our attention from the outside of the circle *back* to the elements inside the circle of control.

Now you're grounding yourself in the Attitude from ACE, by bringing yourself back to the present moment and focusing on what you can control right now, instead of letting yourself get distracted by the past or the future—worrying about what you did before, or what might happen next.

You'll notice in both examples, preparation is key. You *need* that training to fall back on. Without it, no amount of deep breathing or focus is going to help you succeed. That's why practice is so, so important. In the moments when you're feeling overwhelmed, that muscle memory kicks in, you feel like you've done this before, and just like that—you get a little confidence back.

ACE helps with that practice, too. You need the right Attitude, Concentration, and Effort to do those practices and get the most out of them, to plan out your approach in a way that will help you. With things like getting ready for an audition, often there isn't a teacher or adult walking you through it, unless you ask your parents for help. You have to drive yourself forward by making your own practice plan, and setting your own goals and objectives. If you're focused on your Attitude, Concentration, and Effort, chances are you'll choose to focus on the right things, and that practice will be productive naturally.

ACE helps with anxiety by bringing your attitude, concentration, and effort back on the things you can control. Have you gotten the message yet? Like the eye of a hurricane, your worries and anxieties may be flying around outside your circle of control, but your focus is on that still center: the three things you can control. So many times when I talk to athletes about anxiety, I hear that what's making them anxious are the outcomes they're fixated on. *I don't want to let my mom and dad down. I really want to do well.* Those are outcomes, and you can't control them. The ACE method frees you from that pressure to control things that you ultimately can't control, which is at the heart of anxiety. You're placing your attention outside of the circle of control, and it leads to distraction and overwhelm.

CONFIDENCE (AGAIN)

Obviously, anxiety and confidence are polar opposites. Much like performance anxiety, confidence can be related to your focus on outcomes. But performance anxiety is what happens when you focus too much on outcomes, and confidence is what happens when you manage to bring your focus back to that ACE circle of controls.

A lack of confidence is one of the reasons athletes decide to bring in a mental coach. When I start asking them about that lack of confidence, what I hear the most is that they've become fixated on a variety of uncontrollables. They've developed a habit of checking their rankings, or they've become really obsessed about perfecting their technique in their game, or worried about the crowd or game plan of their opponent.

Kevin, a young tennis athlete, was just starting to attract Division I attention and it was starting to mess with his head a little. He started to feel like he needed to be at the top of the rankings, and his tennis serve needed to be going in every time, or he wasn't good enough.

Kevin's lack of confidence comes back to his attitude. He was placing too much importance on things he couldn't control, outcomes like his ranking, whether the Division I schools were happy with him, or whether or not the ball went in after his serve. When it came to his serve, Kevin just needed to work on his technique in order to get better, and to keep a healthy perspective (attitude) that he didn't have to be perfect! Maybe the schools will stay interested, maybe they won't. That's not Kevin's decision. Kevin only can control his attitude, concentration, and effort.

Let's say you're interested in asking someone out. Good chance you may feel nervous, because what if they say no? Now, I realize that most young people have these kinds of conversations over text or social media now. And why not! We can handle rejection a lot easier through a private message compared to around a group of their friends, right? But even if you do it over text, you're still putting yourself out there, and it can still hurt if the other person isn't interested.

In a case like this, you're not confident because you don't know how you'll handle it if they say no. You may have built this person up in your mind as someone you really like, and you're so focused on what it would be like to go on a date with them that you're even more afraid of rejection—it will hurt more because you want this more.

But that's fixating on a future that's not here yet. As much as you can imagine dating this person, and how great it would be, you haven't asked them out yet, so you don't even know for sure if they're interested. That's an important first step! So that future outcome, where they say yes and you go on the date, doesn't exist yet. There's no point in focusing and dreaming on it.

After that, you can go through the W.I.N. exercise. What's important right now?

Is it important that they say yes? Truthfully, no, because you aren't in control of them liking you.

What is important?

Did your message come across the way you wanted it to, to this individual? Did your message say what you wanted it to say? If you thought out your message and they still said no, then you can rest assured knowing you gave your best effort.

CONNECT BACK TO ACE

Remember that this is a human being you're talking to, with their own feelings and their own stuff going on—empathize with them and ask yourself how they will feel about what you're saying, rather than just focusing on your own desire for things to go well. If they reject you, it might hurt but look at it through a growth mindset. Pick one aspect of ACE and dial into it 100%.

As ACE has taught us, you don't control outcomes. And ultimately, the outcome doesn't matter. If they're not interested, they're not interested. It doesn't change anything about you or who you are. So to feel confident, start by adjusting your attitude and perspective. Remind yourself that the outcome isn't what's important. What's important is that you commit and put your full effort into sharing whatever message you want to share with that person in a respectful way.

CONFIDENCE AND WORK

Starting your career and developing it is a really hard thing to do and it takes confidence. Applying for jobs, going to interviews, asking for a raise or a promotion—all of those things require confidence. If you walk into a job interview and you're so nervous you can barely speak, you're not going to leave a great impression on the interviewer. You *need* confidence to stay calm, answer the questions well, and be yourself. Being able to muster confidence when you need to is a really crucial life skill, regardless of where you go in life.

Once you get over the fear of being rejected, cool things start to happen. You develop a toughened mindset. That fear of rejection becomes something that you can filter out, rather than being controlled by. Now you're free to focus on what you can control— yourself. Every single time your focus comes back to ACE, you grow in confidence. Confidence is based on knowing what you can control and not worrying about anything else.

MOTIVATION (AGAIN)

Let's say you've just found out that your mom or dad got a new job and you have to move to a new city. You're going to have to go to a new school and make new friends. Oh, and you need to start packing because you're moving in the next two weeks.

So you go to your room, and you just sit there. You know you're supposed to start packing, or at least think about packing, but you're feeling overwhelmed and completely unmotivated to do anything. How do you wrap your head around this?

With ACE, you start by reminding yourself what you *don't* control Do you control whether or not your family moves? No. So let that go.

Now, take a look at your **attitude**. It's natural to focus on bad news right away, but there's a way to see the positive in this. You don't know what cool things might be about to happen. You might make amazing new friends who you would never have met otherwise.

Concentrate on doing the little things right. You don't control whether or not you make new friends right away in a new place, but you do control how you behave. Show some character and integrity at your new school. Don't just go along with the crowd. Focus on your schoolwork, make connections with the teachers, counselors, or coaches around you as well. Ask questions. Learn about your school. Investigate what things of interest are outside of school. In turn, because of your genuine interest, you may find out that they will ask you about your life and your story as well.

When it comes to **effort**, commit to giving the proper effort every step of the way. Help your parents, because they're going to have a lot on their plates. When you get to the new house, remind yourself that you have the ability to make new friends, and allow yourself to actually put in the effort to talk to people and look for ways to connect.

It can be really scary to reach out to others to try and make new friends. It's a vulnerable moment. In your old town, you probably had friends that you had known for a long time, and it was easy to maintain those relationships. A growth mindset will help. You move to a new place, you don't have friends right away, but you will. They might not come to you—you might have to go to them. Join sports or extracurriculars, introduce yourself to people, be yourself, and you will make friends naturally over time.

When you're in a new social situation, it's easy to dismiss your moral compass and go along with the social crowd to fit in. If you're going to make real friends, you have to be yourself, and that means following your sense of integrity and values. If you know you're doing the right thing, even if you don't have support in that social setting, you'll still have confidence and motivation to keep going.

An elite tennis player, Derek, could be a Division I athlete if he wanted to, but that's the question he's struggling with right now. Does he want to? What's his "why"? He doesn't know right now. How far do you think he'll get when he doesn't have anything driving him? How does it affect his ACE when he doesn't have that basic passion for the sport? Without that, what reason is there for him to do any of this?

What Derek really needs to is figure out is what his values are. What's important to him? What matters? ACE is just a way to help you accomplish your goals. Before ACE can kick in, you need to know what you want to accomplish, and why. Once Derek figures that out, his motivation will come through along with the rest of ACE.

Our first step to understand motivation's root: motive, which means a reason for action. It's the "why". It's the why we do something.

—Brendon Burchard, *The Motivation Manifesto: Nine Declarations to Claim Your Personal Power.*

This is exactly what Derek is struggling with. Motivation comes from having a why, having a reason for action. He needs to understand why he's playing and what he's playing for.

These questions can help you find your motivation in any situation.

To return to the example of moving to a new city and having to make new friends at school, you could ask yourself: *Why do I go to school?* The answer obviously isn't just to hang out with friends. You go to school to get an education and eventually get your high school diploma. Friends are actually secondary.

Once you put that into perspective, you'll experience a whole attitude adjustment. That lack of motivation you felt, the feeling that, *I don't want to go to school today because I don't have any friends,*—that should fade into the background and become secondary. Once you remember your true reason for going to school, you get your motivation back.

Now, sometimes you give yourself a "why" and your motivation still fizzles out. That means it's time to dig a little deeper. For example, if Derek decides that he wants to play tennis so that he can make all-conference and all-state selections, that's a good start. But it's a motivation that's outside of him, it's based on an outcome. When the season is over and he went all-conference or all-state, what's Derek's motivation going to be for the offseason? Keep reaching Derek!

Once you know your "why," you can also start to outline the steps you need to take.

We also lose motivation sometimes because the problems we need to solve just feel so huge, like Derek trying to figure out his reason for playing sports. It's a huge question to ask! How do you even start solving it?

Well, ACE is a broad idea, too. There are so many ways to apply and interpret it in your life.

If you were to physically stretch your arms as wide as possible, that's how big ACE is. The uncontrollables that we face sometimes, can feel even bigger. But what I'm asking you to do as an athlete is to bring your arms together so they form a circle, and your fingers are just touching. That's your circle of control. It's small and manageable. That's the area you're responsible for. That's where your focus should be.

In other words, when you're facing a huge problem and you don't even know where to start, a key technique for finding motivation is to narrow your focus. What's one thing you can do, right now, that would help you start tackling your big problems? It might be as small as making a list of the things you need to do, or scheduling a time to talk to your coach about some of the issues you might be facing. Those tiny tasks can give you just enough momentum to keep going to the next task, and the next one.

Small progress is still progress.

If you're moving to a new place and you don't know how to make new friends, you can start to find your motivation by looking for small improvements, building winning behaviors, every day. Can you make a small improvement to your attitude each day? Can you introduce yourself to a new person, or try a new activity at school, each day? Once you get those small things going, you'll start to see the next step forward. Anyone can do this and see a significant improvement over time.

TWO MONKS

Two monks were on a quest, passing through one village to the next to return to their monastery. During the course of their journey, they approached a river they needed to cross. To their surprise, they saw a woman lying next to the river, barely breathing and barely alive.

Her clothes were torn and tattered and she was fading in and out of consciousness, whispering, "Help me. Please, help me." The monks both looked at each other, and then back at the woman. One of the monks knew there was a village nearby, across the river, where they could help the woman. He began to bend down and pick her up.

The other monk quickly grabbed him by the arm and shouted, "You took a vow, brother, to never touch a woman. Does your promise mean nothing?"

The first monk brushed off the other's hands, bent over, picked the woman up in his arms, and began to wade across the river with the other monk trailing close behind. The two monks continued walking until they found the village up ahead. They brought the woman to an inn, and she received immediate care. The two monks then continued on their quest for a long period of silence. The monk who had tried to prevent the other from picking up the woman said to him belligerently, "Brother, we both vowed never to touch a woman. You not only touched her, but you carried her in your arms. How could you?"

And without hesitation, the other monk smiled, and replied, "Brother, I quit carrying that woman hours and miles ago. Why do you still carry her?"

In other words, that monk focused on what was important in the moment. He knew his vow wasn't important in that moment, only the human life in front of him. In contrast, his fellow monk had spent the entire time focused on the wrong thing and was so distracted by it that it was still troubling him a long time later, long after they left the woman behind.

GOAL SETTING/GETTING

VALUE

I asked Alicia, a Division I coach, about her goals, and her team's goals, for the season. She told me she had been doing some reading and decided that goals aren't necessarily a good thing. I realize this may be a trend in the sports community, but with all due respect to authors who advocate for this point of view, goals are a proven tool for success.

Sport Psychology has established that goals increase motivation and performance, and they support a better sense of fulfilment, motivation, and accomplishment in whatever we're doing. Once you set a goal, you've created something to measure your progress against. Even if you don't make it all the way there, you'll be able to see some kind of improvement, or worst case scenario…feedback! When you set out on a journey there is change constantly happening! This feedback helps us stay motivated. When you do reach that goal, you get this wonderful sense of accomplishment. Even if you were taking the same steps to improve, working on the same things, but without a specific goal, you might not get that same sense of recognition and satisfaction.

Here are my top 5 reasons why goal-getting works:

1. Goals direct our attention
2. They help direct our efforts and keep us plugged in and disciplined
3. Goals take time to achieve—we must be persistent in chasing them
4. Goals provide feedback! Have a big goal? Great. Failed at it? Try a new way. Failed again? Try again. Get back up and keep going. Keep trying new strategies until one works!
5. We can track and measure how we're doing easily by looking into the progress we're making towards goals

So I encouraged and assisted setting goals with Alicia and her team. We set goals by determining the outcome we wanted to see and then working backward through the steps that would need to happen in order for that bigger goal to happen. Those smaller steps are called "process goals".

EXPLAIN BEYOND SPORTS

Unsurprisingly, some of the best advice I ever received on achieving goals came from a friend of mine who happens to be a Navy SEAL. He had made it through BUDS training, an elite course that has an approximate 80% attrition or failure rate. One of the instructors' favorite things to tell the new classes is to run to the ocean and become a "sugar cookie". You run into the Pacific Ocean, which is cold year-round, fully submerge yourself and get soaking wet. Then you run back onto the beach and roll around in the dry sand until you're completely covered with sand on every inch of your body. You then run up a nearby hill, and when you get to the top, instructors may bellow personal insults and instructions at you. You may get to the top of the hill, and they tell you to turn around and run straight back into the water. You may do this over and over again.

All the while, an instructor is talking calmly on a megaphone saying things like, "This sucks. I wonder what my family is doing. I wonder if I'll make it up the hill again. My legs hurt. I need a nap. I am about to quit." The messaging goes on and on, encouraging these candidates to quit and drop out. This is a big mind game.

Here were his tips:

1. **Embrace the suck.** There's a visualization technique for this. You picture whatever you're trying to do as a big scary monster. The scarier it is, the more intimidating that goal or objective is for you. Then imagine yourself embracing that monster, literally—giving it a big hug or kiss. Just to let it know that it doesn't scare you. ***For the record, he also said that once you give it a big kiss on the cheek, you slap it on the butt and keep going.***

2. **Play the game.** Elite training is designed to break you down mentally, physically, emotionally, and also through sleep. It seems intense and scary, but it's all a carefully designed game that the instructors are playing to wear you down, and you can play it too. When you treat something like a game, you look for small wins, strategies, any little thing you can do to make it easier. So turn your big scary goals into a game.

3. **Eat an elephant one bite at a time.** When your goal is really huge and scary, it's easy to become completely overwhelmed. If you let yourself think about how big and scary the objective is, you'll never get there. If you're doing the "sugar cookie" and you let yourself start thinking about how long those 30 minutes are going to feel, you'll run out of energy before you even become a cookie for the second time. Instead, focus on the next tiny step of the way. One step at a time, one bite at a

time, never stopping to think about the whole thing, just the next little bit.

I'm sure you can see the pattern here. The secret to goal-getting is to break your objective into bite-size pieces and go after them one at a time.

For example, let's say you want to do really well on your SAT. Maybe you have a specific score or a range that you'd like to get. That's your overall goal. The next step is to figure out the things that need to happen in order to get there. You'll probably need to do a prep class, you might want a tutor. You might have a teacher you can work with to prepare outside of class, with tests and timed assignments. Now you've broken your big goal down into manageable chunks. And you can break those down even further into to-do lists, if you do well with lists. If you want to take an SAT prep class, you'll need to do the work to find a good course, figure out the logistics such as dates and fees, and get everything all lined up to take the course.

CONNECT BACK TO ACE

To approach goals, again, you really need an ACE mindset. If you don't reach your goal, you need the right Attitude to either adjust the goal or figure out what you can do better on next time. You need the right Concentration to prioritize the tasks that are the most important for your goal, and of course, the right Effort to actually execute on your plans and put in the work.

You can see, goal-setting goes way beyond just picking something that you want to see happen. "I want to do well on the SATs" is a good start, but there's still more work to do. You have to break that goal down into the process goals and keep an eye on your progress, so you know if you need to make adjustments.

Once you have your goal and process goals, you need to link it back to your values, your "why".

For example, if you have a goal to get a good SAT score, it's probably because you're looking to go to an great or prestigious school. If you start that process to get the SAT score you're after, and you find you're not doing well in the prep class or on the practice tests, then it's time to sit back and figure out what's going wrong. Part of this can be your values. Why is going to an elite academic school important to you? If you really think about it, you might find that it's actually not. Maybe it's a goal your parents set for you and you're trying to carry it out, but you actually want something very different. Maybe you want to go to a local school, or a sports-focused school. If that's the case, your motivation will be off as you're pursuing that prestigious academic school, because that goal doesn't actually align with your values.

Another example is weight loss. Many people set a goal to lose 10 or 20 pounds, but just a few weeks into the new diet or exercise plan, most of us tend to lose motivation. Why? Because we feel pressure to lose weight, but we haven't connected it to our own values. We haven't given it a deep "why" analysis. If you connect it to something specific, like *I want to look good for my friend's wedding, I want to make it up a flight of stairs without getting out of breath, I want to be able to do pull-ups,* all of a sudden it's much more immediate and meaningful. That "why" boosts your motivation. Can you find something deeper and more meaningful than those reasons though? Can I challenge you to dig deeper and identify what would losing this weight mean for you? Mean for your health? Mean for those around you? Don't ever be afraid to dig in and go deeper.

Money is another area where most of us mean well but quickly lose motivation. How many times have you looked at what you're spending on fast food or entertainment, and thought to yourself, *I should just stop. This is an easy thing to give up and I'll save so much money!* But a month or two later, you're back to your old habits.

The first two letters of goal are go. So, where are you trying to go? Is there a vacation or a big purchase you want to make? What's the reason for this goal—why is it so important? Once you have that, you'll be able to figure out the rest, even if it means staying home instead of going out or giving up one of your takeout meals a month.

If your goal doesn't have a specific "why", but you know it's a good thing to do, then the "why" can simply be change and growth. Change is inevitable. I've learned this the hard way by noticing the tiny wrinkles starting to form around my eyes at the ripe old age of 31. Change is completely unavoidable, but growth is 100% optional.

Change is like a river. It has a current, and you can try to paddle against it, but you're going to exhaust yourself and not get very far. So, you can't fight the current forever, but you can choose the direction downstream where you go. Which bank of the river do you want to get to? How far do you want to go? Do something to shape where you end up, instead of sitting in your canoe feeling helpless. As obstructions come up in the river, you can choose how to direct yourself. Instead of getting stuck, you can push off that rock and use it to get yourself where you need to go.

BURNOUT [2]

Burnout is defined as "physical or mental collapse, caused by overwork or stress".

I have seen this condition in many athletes and experienced it myself. I was playing for a coach in a toxic environment, and I just ran out of steam. I was giving my all, not receiving recognition, and it was too much stress for too little benefit. Most of us can handle a period of stress if it's for some larger goal, or we know it will lead to something better. What tends to break us is when we feel it's for nothing, or just for someone else's ego.

I encountered another type of burnout once when I was speaking to a multi-millionaire, Dave. Dave could buy a small country if he wants to. He's extremely successful, but he hated what he was doing. He would have liked to stop, but just didn't feel he could walk away. Burnout like that is like a mosquito that keeps sucking your blood, and you let it, even though you know it's draining you.

Burnout doesn't discriminate. Billionaires and broke people can both get burnt out. Elite performers, and people who don't feel they have any particular talent. There's burnout from working too hard, or not working hard enough if you have a job that's extremely boring. You can experience religious burnout, emotional burnout... any area

---

[2]Disclaimer: I am not a counselor or psychologist. The advice in this book does not represent professional psychological advice. If you are experiencing mental health issues, you should speak to a licensed professional.

of your life that requires effort, you can get burnt out from doing it in a way that's not good for you.

CONNECT BACK TO ACE

Looking back, during my university years, my sophomore and junior years athletically I was burned out playing for my head coach and program, but I still loved the sport of baseball and I still wanted to help others. I eventually gave up my last year of baseball eligibility (my 5th year due to a freshman redshirt) because of this burnout. Looking back, I had a very weak mental foundation of ACE. If I could go back in time, I'd coach myself on redirecting my focus back to those things that I still loved, and that would have significantly helped me recover quicker from my burnout and the feelings I had developed.

Niko was a first-time Olympic swimmer from a Pacific Island country I will not name, and he was feeling pressure from home and pressure from his country's federation. He was training with us at the Olympic site I worked at in Northeast Ohio and it was a whole new level of training for him. He was just in the beginning stages of burnout, where he was starting to check out mentally. He had stopped taking joy in his sport.

To help Niko with his burnout, we imposed a two-week timeout and we spent that time focusing on everything and anything but sports. We realigned his ACE and refreshed his values. We looked at what it means to be an athlete. We watched motivational documentaries to learn about other athletes. We continued doing workouts and training because it turned out Niko still wanted to work out, he just wasn't used to being in the water as much as his coach had him doing. All of this was intended to rebuild Niko's passion and energy for the sport.

After two weeks, Niko was itching to get back in the water. He went through his first swimming practice in two weeks, and afterward, he told his coach and myself, "I feel like a brand-new person."

"I used to just focus on how everything seemed like too much—over-practicing, overtraining. Now I feel like it's a privilege to swim.

I'm lucky to be able to swim. I feel excited and proud of what I can do." In those two weeks, Niko had unlearned the old habits of thinking that led to his burnout. He had developed a completely new way of thinking about his sport. It's worth mentioning that while this is an example of a quick turnaround, not all results happen this quick on this topic.

When you look at burnout from an ACE perspective, I can see it as an imbalance of the elements. Maybe it's too much effort for what you're getting out of it, or your concentration has become too narrow on one tiny aspect of the game, or your attitude has suffered because of circumstances around you, and you haven't found a way to adjust.

What's really interesting about dealing with burnout is that it clears the way for something new. Like a forest fire, it burns up all of the debris and distractions, leaving empty space for a new seed to grow. Like with Niko's time-out, you can take the opportunity to clear out all of your old habits and see what comes to take its place. In the end, the forest is much the same—all the big trees are still there because they survived the fire. But there's something new growing, and over time, that forest will come to look completely different.

THE GROUND RULES

1. Be prepared to re-evaluate old habits and assumptions.
2. Don't be afraid to disagree. Critical thinking is an important part of this process.
3. Be determined, patient and consistent; it may take time to see results once you start applying these concepts.
4. Maintain an open, teachable mind.
5. Empty your cup.

LIVING YOUR BEST ACE LIFE!

In this journey you've likely heard many things that may be new for the first time. We covered a lot of ground. Many times, when I first teach ACE to athletes or groups, although how simple it is, its information overload. Sometimes I've found that the simplest ideas or simplest stories offers the best wisdom or can be deeply profound.

There's a formula that I've adopted and used over the years that helps athletes and individuals reflect back in on their performance and how they've done quickly and effectively. It was taught to me as the WBL chart or the "Well, Better, Learned" chart and list.

Within this summary, I'd like to invite you with me to reflect on where you've been through this journey of understanding how ACE can impact and transform your athletic career and personal life.

My suggestion to get the most out of this, would be to brainstorm the following on a three-tiered chart like below and fill it out.

WELL

As an athlete, list the top three traits that you do well on a steady and consistent basis. What areas are you complimented on? Are you a good teammate? Do you bring a consistent energy to your sport? Perhaps your mindset? Thankful for opportunities that are given to you? List your top three qualities that you do well.

BETTER

Time to reflect after learning about ACE and I encourage you to list three things that you need to be better at. Think broad as it relates to the circle of control. Do we need to improve on letting go of the desire to be perfect? Need to let go of 'controlling' our results? How about other's opinions? What about our nutrition, sleep, or even stretching? Stretch yourself here and identify three things you need to be better at.

LEARNED

If you applied the rules of each chapter prior to reading, there's a great chance that you have a wonderful opportunity to take several messages out of here that you can apply immediately. What did you learn throughout this journey? Did you pick up any new strategies that you could apply to your training, competition, or life?

A large ship is controlled by such a small rudder. A small shift in the direction of the rudder and a small shift in mindset may help lead you in a completely new trajectory than you previously thought possible.

**Take a few moments and fill out the
WBL chart on the next page.**

WELL	BETTER	LEARNED
1.	1.	1.
2.	2.	2.
3.	3.	3.

Reflecting on the athletes I have worked with in the past, many of their problems, challenges, and issues arise by consciously or subconsciously allowing our attention being focused on the outside of the circle. Athletes largely get into trouble when the things on the outside become more important than the things on the inside.

Can we agree on that?

If you're honest and open we have to admit that from time to time we have things that seek to steal and rob our attention, our energy, and at times our beliefs and values. The circle of control ACE is a simple tool used as a reminder that we can always direct our attention back to the circle and place the importance of our focus and energy on one of those three aspects.

I learned ACE during the fall of 2011 but didn't fully understand it until the spring of 2014. As I write this now even in 2019, I am constantly reminded weekly of how constant ACE is. It's in everything that is happening around me, the athletes and individuals and families I work with, my personal and family life, and how we are constantly reacting and responding to adversities and blessings.

I've always felt a deeper connection to ACE.

It began during 2014 while I was working at SPIRE Institute (U.S. Olympic & Paralympic Training Site). Yes, I'd been living the best version of an ACE life as I could as I had learned it, but I was after a deeper meaning and it led me to a place of prayer and reflection.

A wise friend, mentor, and man who's discipled me in my Christian faith over the years shared something during 2014 that I cannot shake. I can hear his raspy full of wisdom voice right now, "Trevor, there are a few things that all mankind is born with…one of those being—we are all born with a *strong desire* and sense of *autonomy* and *control*. Another is a sense of *justice*. Third we live daily based on *faith*."

THE FIRST TRUTH: AUTONOMY AND CONTROL

No one has taught my two-year-old how to lie and to be motivated by his own self-interests. "Gabriel, did you eat the cookie?" Gabriel with his mouth full of crumbs, and his mouth still full of the cookie he's chewing, looks at me with big eyes and shakes his head sharply **no**. As funny as that example is, it's true *(mankind wanted to know "Truth"—read about the fall of man in Genesis chapter 3)*.

THE SECOND TRUTH: A SENSE OF JUSTICE

It is easy to point to any example on the news right now and be outraged over something. We live in a snap judgment society where we want the "bad guys/other side" punished for their crimes, or held accountable for something said, or something done. If justice isn't strong enough, or it doesn't go to our liking, we have a natural reaction of hurt and can lead to feeling victimized.
(Ecclesiastes 3:17)

THE THIRD TRUTH: FAITH

This one may sound strange at first, but let's define it. Faith is simply commitment before knowing (Hebrews 11:1 NASB).

I challenge you also to think about this from a non-religious point of view. When you pull up to the McDonalds drive thru window to order your double cheeseburger, you have faith that the meat has been properly cooked, and you're not going to get sick by eating that sandwich. You're committing (to eat) before knowing (food poisoning or not).

Here's another example. We've heard that airplanes are safer form of transportation than driving a vehicle. If you're about to hop on that plane, before heading to your seat, you interview the pilot and say, "Mr. Pilot, can you guarantee me that we are going to arrive safely at our destination?"

Pilot: "Well, young man, the sun is out, perfect visibility, and our plane is in great shape to fly, I feel very confident (smiling) we're going to get to our destination."

You: "Can you 100% guarantee me?"

Pilot: "Hm…well…how does 99.999% certainty work?"

Remember 99.999% does not equal 100% does it?

At that moment, when you decide to head to your seat, you put your full faith—literal definition—into the pilot and co-pilot to take you and all the other passengers and crew to the destination.

LET'S REVIEW

1. Mankind is born with a sense of autonomy and desire of control.
2. We desire a sense of justice.
3. We all live by faith (commitment before knowing).

If you're not a Christian reading this, I encourage you to test the principle of ACE on the merits of the simplicity it brings. ACE much like competition and living day to day relies on faith. Commitment before knowing.

Perhaps when my mentor used the word 'control' it clicked. You see, I had been applying the ACE principles of "Control what you can Control" for about three years at that point, and it was at that moment that I instantly understood the deeper connection that I could never put my thumb on it.

Bottom line: Man is **not** in control.

We tend to think our way is best, yet we utterly fail time and time again in multiple aspects of our life.

Questions for you to reflect on:
1. How did you look at the world around you *before* reading this book?
2. How do you look at the world around you *now*?
3. What lens do you *choose* to look through when the world knocks you to your knees?
4. In the past, when things spiralled out of control, how quick did you refocus on your Attitude, Concentration, or Effort?
5. Understanding ACE now, how quick *will* you be to refocus now?
6. Are you comfortable admitting and accepting that you're not in control?
7. Are you ready to let go of trying to control and manipulate the world and events around you?

It took years for me to admit that and to let go. Remember from the beginning my challenge to you…

This book from the beginning was never about learning. It's about understanding.

Understanding is the first step towards mastery. You can begin mastering the simple formula of ACE.
1. *Understand* and *Apply* ACE in your **personal life *and*** your **sport life**—they are connected at the hip!
2. Turn ACE into your best weaponized *habit* you have—this is both mental and physical. Trust me, your opponents don't think this way…but that doesn't mean that you can't.
3. Model ACE! When others look at you and the way you live and react to life's adversities, you can choose your perspective and others will notice! "I'm not in control, but I'm choosing how to respond."

A FINAL WISH FOR YOU MY READER:

May the formula of ACE permeate every aspect of your life. I pray that ACE can lead you to new horizons, journeys, and places that you cannot even fathom. Keep in mind my friend, the circumstances and pleasures of this world are destined to let you down. A life with deep roots of ACE will not.

I wish you abundant blessings to you for choosing this journey of ACE.

APPENDIX

ACE AND ME

I'll save some pages on how I got to own a consulting business and instead I'll point directly to the source: divine intervention. I was over a year and a half into my Master's degree in Guidance & Counseling when I realized that working in a school the rest of my life was something I wasn't so keen on anymore. Dr. Linda Sterling, a wonderful professor of mine, asked me where my heart was at. I shared with her about how I was keen on continuing with athletics after my college baseball career abruptly ended. She persuaded and encouraged me to apply for the Mental Conditioning Internship program at IMG Academy in Bradenton, Florida.

I loved working with students in a guidance counseling school setting, and loved the opportunity to make an impact, but I reached a point where I just felt I wasn't doing that in the most direct way. I was already an athlete and coach, and I wanted to help people through a new lens—through mental conditioning.

I first heard the term "mental conditioning" from a Tony Robbins audiotape, *Anthony Robbins Personal Power: A 30 Day Program*, that my father owned, copyrighted 1996. Tony speaks about mental conditioning, referencing the importance of conditioning your mind.

In J*ust ACE It!*, mental conditioning refers to a profession (Mental Conditioning Coach). An MC is someone who helps others train mentally to reach their peak performance.

I first encountered the idea of using psychology in my own life during my redshirt year at my university. During my redshirt freshman fall ball season, the upperclassmen and my teammates were processing the games and practice quicker than I was. I could no doubt hold my own, but some of these guys were thinking differently about the game.

After fall ball season, coaches will sit each player down for individual meetings. Some guys are cut from the team, some find out they're not going to be traveling in the spring time and they are free to transfer out, and some, like me, find out that they are getting redshirted. If you're not familiar with the term "redshirt", it is when you're on a varsity baseball team, sometimes that athlete is on scholarship, and the NCAA allows you to practice, but not to play competitions (except inter-squad scrimmages and games). This can happen for a variety of reasons, but the point is, I wasn't happy about it. I essentially took it as "I'm not good enough". I spent the next 6 months upset, believing that my teammates were improving while I was sitting on the sidelines.

That spring, I started taking to online self-study. I switched my major from biology pre-med to psychology. I had already identified these guys were thinking the game quicker than I was... so I knew I had to be better mentally. I made the connection eventually, after being upset for months, that you could think the game better, even if you weren't playing. Talk about what's in your control, right!?

I continued through my undergraduate program and graduated with a 4-year degree in 4 years (which I'm still proud of!) and was accepted into the graduate school's counseling program I mentioned earlier. I had one year of eligibility left to play baseball but ended up walking away from a 5th year of eligibility. Burnout experienced from a program and a head coach.

I wish I had the ACE method then! After leaving baseball as an athlete, I began my coaching career. The whole time, I kept up with my self-study; reading books, listening to CDs, anything I could get my hands on. I was hooked on the mental game and how it could improve your performance. Essentially, I was on a journey of self-discovery, trying to learn everything I could about the mind.

The internship in Florida was a program where I was up against Master's and Doctoral candidates applying from Sport Psychology or Counseling Psychology related disciplines, where some of them were even published authors and already had experience working in the field professionally! I didn't think I had any business trying to compete with candidates like that, but I gave it a shot anyway. As part of the application process, I had to present a video of myself teaching a skill. I sent in a video of a team building activity I did with the team I was working with at the time. You could see on the kids' faces that they were connecting with the material; they were experiencing something real. That tape got me an interview, and then I was accepted, and that's how I ended up on the IMG campus, at that session, listening to Dr. Angus Mugford explain the ACE concept briefly to tennis players.

I could point to several defining moments of my career; however, the most transformative moments happened working on campus at IMG. In the Mental Conditioning program, I was constantly challenged in my delivery and approach to educating athletes.

The revelation in my life, and for the lives of the people I teach, comes from realizing that ACE can be applied to anything in your life. It doesn't have to be a sport. It doesn't have to be limited to challenging or difficult circumstances. I was learning to find my own path, to self-actualize, and I quickly realized that if I could do it, anyone could. This method could help anyone.

Even as I was completing that fall internship, I was encountering difficulties and stressors. I was working consistent 50- to 60-hour weeks—we all were (interns)—with only my room and board covered, and nothing else. I had student loans; I had a Master's degree waiting for my return from the Florida hiatus. All of us interns had other bills to pay. I would hear other interns complaining about all of the work they had to do—and in fairness it was a lot, but they knew what they signed up for. I've never been one for drama, but it was upsetting hearing the ungrateful attitudes expressed from some of my intern colleagues. I was drawn immediately back to this thought, "This is ACE right here. You choose your attitude Trevor, don't let these other people choose it for you. There's only a few things that are in your control. The rest of it isn't, so don't worry about that. Focus on ACE."

It started with small habits: choosing to get up earlier than my roommates so I could have alone time to focus and reset. I worked at it and got my morning down to a science in a matter of days. If I set the alarm at 6:05AM, I ate my oatmeal by 6:15AM, I got in the shower by 6:25AM before anyone was stirring. I made it a priority to be the first one up, first one out with the goal to have left the apartment by 6:45AM (before the other guys had even heard their alarms).

I would walk to campus early in the morning, setting aside any drama or negativity, being fully present, conscious and aware of choosing my thoughts and my attitude as well as making time for a moment of quick prayer. That simple decision to get up early transformed my experience of the internship. I didn't complain like the others did, because it didn't feel like work to me. I was choosing my path through the forest, enjoying the beauty of the experience, and the others around me just seemed to be lost among the trees.

Seeing the impact these changes had in in my life, compared to the experiences of my peers, nagged at me. I wanted to follow that path further and see how far it went. How could this simple idea be so transformational?

As the internship program was winding down, completing my Master's degree was a priority. Our university had nationally ranked tennis programs both on the men's and women's side, so I decided to cold-call the tennis coach and asked if he had a graduate assistant (GA) position open.

It was my priority to obtain my degree in Guidance & Counseling, and I knew in my heart that I wanted to work in this mental conditioning field. The coach shared that he already had a GA. Disappointing. About three weeks before the semester was to start, I received a call. My heart skipped a beat on it: "The GA I had lined up bailed on me. Trevor, I'm willing to give you a one semester try-out of this 'mental conditioning' you speak of, if you're up for it."

The next two years flew by. That's right. I passed the try-out, helping take our men's team to a national tournament and on to win the conference tournament 2 years in a row.

The NCAA Division II national tournament was held in Phoenix, Arizona (May, 2013) our team was eliminated first round from the tournament and just qualifying to get there was a heck of an accomplishment. We chose to stay and watch the next day's quarter-final matches. I looked down while watching another match and received this text:

"Hi, Trevor. My name's Chad Bohling. I'm the Mental Conditioning Director for the New York Yankees. I hear you may be interested in a job, and I'm reaching out on behalf of looking to help someone fill a role/position in Ohio."

My jaw dropped. I'm pretty sure I turned pale. Working at IMG I had heard Dr. Angus and a few colleagues mention Chad's name from time to time so I thought to myself, what in the world would possess Chad to reach out to me!

That text seemed to fall out of the sky, but the truth is, it was an answer to prayer. I had been praying hard, for about a month in March spring, to find a job in the field of mental conditioning.

One day, on my way to campus for class, I hopped in my truck and started to drive. As I pulled up to a stop sign, I found myself in prayer and surrendering the whole question to God with my career decision and the inevitable question of, "Lord, what do I do after I graduate? It's 2 months away...and right now I've got nothing." I said, "God, hey. You know what? I don't know what's going on. I don't know what you've got for me but tell you what. I'm going to quit worrying about this job search. I'm going to start living ACE again. I'm going to leave it up to you."

Instantly, like a strike of lightning, a song came on the radio. It was "Don't You Worry, Child" by Swedish House Mafia, and it was playing the chorus: "Don't you worry, don't you worry, child. Heaven's got a plan for you." I started to cry, laughing, wiping my tears through my sunglasses, overwhelmed with the message of that song and that moment. Divine intervention.

In June (2013), I was offered a position as a school counselor in Missouri. It paid well and had great benefits. But I prayed about it, and I felt God was leading me somewhere else, so I turned it down. That was a tough decision. It was a very good job, and I was back living with my parents at the time of this transition. Two degrees, student loans, and first great job comes my way and I turn it down. Although my parents didn't say it, I'm sure they were thinking it... "What are you thinking, kid?" They were always asking for an update on how my job hunt was going and if I had any leads. The day I told them I received a good job offer and turned it down, I could feel the concern on their faces.

Chad and I had been in touch since May as he was helping screen and interview me for this opportunity in Ohio that was developing. The job was at SPIRE Institute a US Olympic and Paralympic Site in Geneva, Ohio. Truth be told, a dream opportunity for me. The job was going to grant me the opportunity for me to build my own mental conditioning program working with athletes in a very similar boarding academy setting such as IMG. I was just 26. It was the opportunity of a lifetime, and everything that had happened, all those choices and moments that I didn't understand at the time, just fell into place. Like I said: Divine Intervention.

SPIRE was a dream job and opportunity but in time the Lord led our family to Kansas City for a short two years where I spent those years learning the in-s and out-s of being self-employed in this industry. Talk about a wake-up call. At one point, I remember banging my head against the wall because nothing was working. I wasn't picking up enough new athletes, I wasn't working with nearly enough businesses as I hoped, and I told Erica verbatim, "Hun, I think I have workplace depression… nothing is working!"

Erica being a competitor and my rock, looked at me, sharply turned to me and said, "Quit feeling sorry for yourself, stop focusing on the outcomes or lack of them, and re-focus on ACE. You teach it…get back to living it!"

Ouch.

But she was right. I was worried and so focused on the results and the "no's" and the circumstances (outside the circle of control folks…!) that my ACE was on shaky ground. My solution turned to re-focusing my energy on my business plan, and daily working to improve my attitude and outlook on my situation.

In August of 2017 Hurricane Harvey made landfall in Southeast Texas, and parts of Louisiana dumping an unprecedented amount of rain. Significant parts and segments of Houston flooded. Mind you, Erica and I had made the decision that we were going to move to Houston approximately two weeks before Harvey arrived. We watched in horror, as people were being evacuated and entire communities were wiped out. We looked at each other wondering if it's too late for us to look at another city to move to. Unfortunately, we were moving because of Erica's job and due to our commitment, it was already too late. Enter in ACE.

Since relocating to Houston, I've started from scratch again, building a mental conditioning practice (Hearts & Minds, LLC.) from the ground up, and with some more head banging moments against the wall, my ACE is stronger. I've had new areas of my life to practice it in. I've always thought that there should be a "P" added to that acronym. Patience and prayer. It seems that both of those are also in our ability to control and have significant impact in our daily living.

My business now has taken a new and exciting turn to launch and bring "The Just ACE It Academy" to build on the concepts and foundations illustrated in this book. You can learn more about it through my website www.hmperform.com. It's about creating a virtual one of a kind small group classroom and atmosphere. Individuals who graduate from this program will be #1: more confident, and #2: more consistent in their day to day performances.

It has always intrigued me that some of the greatest challenges' athletes face are so similar, and I've always wanted to create a virtual classroom to connect that swimmer from Fiji, with the soccer athlete from the UK, and the basketball stud that I'm working with in Minnesota.

Performance is performance, and stress is stress no matter how you cut it.

ACE is applicable in any performance and is applicable in any situation. Including business and the adult world.

ACE has been a bedrock principle for the past eight years in my life, and the mission that lies before me is to share to each of you how you too can re-direct your attention and energy from the things that is out of your control to the things that are directly in *your* own circle of influence.

Don't take my word for it.
Test it out for yourself.
I challenge you!

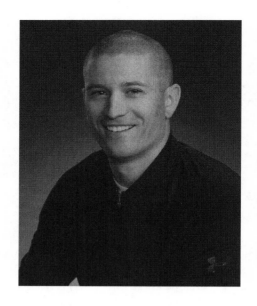

ABOUT TREVOR CONNER

Trevor is a trained mental conditioning coach with over eight years of experience in sports and performance coaching. Through his consulting business, Hearts and Minds, Trevor helps everyone from amateur to Olympic and Professional athletes, to C-suite executives, and to special forces soldiers take control of their performance.

If this book has inspired you in some way, I'd love to hear from you, and learn your story, and what this simple concept has done for you.

You can contact me here:
Email: trevor@hmperform.com
Twitter: @trevorconnermc
Instagram: @tconnermc2

Made in the USA
Columbia, SC
16 November 2020